115 Greatest Caribbean Recipes

of All Time

A Cookbook of Popular West Indian Cuisine

from 26 Caribbean Islands

By

Grace Barrington-Shaw

More books by Grace-Barrington-Shaw:

Copyright © 2017 by Grace Barrington-Shaw. All Rights Reserved

This document is geared toward providing exact and reliable information in regard to the topic and issue covered. The publication is sold with the idea that the publisher is not required to render accounting, officially permitted, or otherwise, qualified services. If advice is necessary, legal or professional, a practiced individual in the profession should be ordered.

- From a Declaration of Principles which was accepted and approved equally by a committee of the American Bar Association and a Committee of Publishers and Associations.

In no way is it legal to reproduce, duplicate or transmit any part of this document in either electronic means or in printed format. Recording of this publication is strictly prohibited and any storage of this document is not allowed unless with written permission from the publisher. All rights reserved.

The information provided herein is stated to be truthful and consistent, in that any liability, in terms of inattention or otherwise, by any usage or abuse of any polices, processes, or directions contained within is the solitary and utter responsibility of the recipient reader. Under no circumstances will any legal responsibility or blame be held against the publisher for any reparation, damages, or monetary loss due to the information herein, either directly or indirectly.

Respective authors own all copyrights not held by the publisher.

The information herein is offered for informational purposes solely, and is universal as so. The presentation of the information is without contract or any guarantee assurance.

The trademarks that are used are without any consent and the publication of the trademark is without permission or backing by trademark owner. All trademarks and brands within this book are for clarifying purposes only and are owned by the owners themselves, not affiliated with this document.

Disclaimer

All reasonable efforts have been made to provide accurate and error-free recipes within this book. These recipes are intended for use by persons possessing the appropriate technical skill, at their own discretion and risk. It is advisable that you take full note of the ingredients before mixing and use substitutes where necessary, to fit your dietary requirements.

Contents

Introduction 10
   FREE Bonuses 16

Anguilla 17
   1. Anguillan Chicken Sausage 17
   2. Crispy Lobster and Vegetable Spring Roll with Soya Lobster Dressing 19
   3. Grilled Chicken Parts with Barbecue Sauce 21
   4. Lemon Herb Butter 23
   5. Lobster Cakes with Tartar Sauce 24
   6. Lobster Pancakes 27
   7. Stuffed Chicken Breast 31
   8. Warm Chocolate Pie 33

Antigua and Barbuda 34
   9. Black Angel Hair Fritters 34
   10. Conch Fritters 36
   11. Ducuna 38
   12. Papaya Pie 40
   13. Pineapple Trifle 42
   14. Pork Chops with Banana and Bacon 44

Aruba 46
   15. Bolita di Keshi 46
   16. Arepa 48
   17. Balchi di Pisca 50
   18. Banana den Forno 52
   19. Bitterbal (Meat Croquettes) 53

Bahamas 54

    20. Bahama Papa 54

    21. Sky Juice 55

    22. Goombay Smash 56

    23. Lionfish Tacos 57

Barbados 59

    24. Cou cou 59

    25. Flying Fish 61

    26. Salt Bread 62

    27. Cutters 64

    28. Fish Cakes 67

British Virgin Islands 68

    29. Baked Crab 68

    30. Garlic Pork 69

    31. Lobster Salad 71

    32. Meat Pate 72

    33. Okra Fungi 74

    34. Rasta Pasta 75

Cayman Islands 77

    35. Seared Lionfish with Tropical Fruit Chutney 77

    36. Cayman Triangle 79

Cuba 81

    37. Medianoche 81

    38. Ropa Vieja 83

    39. Pernil Asado Con Mojo 85

    40. Fricase de Pollo 87

    41. Cubano 89

42. Pescao en Escabeche 91

43. Elena Ruz 93

44. Torticas de Moron 94

Curacao 96

45. Kolo Stoba 96

46. Bolo di Glas 98

47. Banana Stoba 100

48. Bonchi Kora 102

49. Pastechi 104

50. Papaya Stoba 106

51. Balchi di Karni 108

52. Tutu 111

53. Repa di Pampuna 113

Dominica and Dominican Republic 115

54. Sancocho 115

55. Mangu 118

56. Arroz Blanco 120

57. Habichuelas Guisadas 122

58. Pollo Guisado 124

59. Ensalada Verde 126

60. Tostones 128

61. Habichuelas con Dulce 130

Grenada 132

62. Callaloo Soup 132

63. Lambie Souse 134

64. Peleau 136

65. Cocoa Tea 138

66. Sweet Potato Pone 140

67. Nutmeg Ice Cream 142

Guadeloupe **144**

68. Black Bean Chicken 144

69. Caribbean Ginger Turkey 146

70. Pineapple Chicken Rundown 148

71. Stuffed Cabbage Leaves 149

Haiti **151**

72. Poule en Sauce 151

73. Bannann Bouyi 153

74. Espageti 154

75. Sos Pwa 156

Jamaica **158**

76. Jerk Chicken 158

77. Curry Goat 160

78. Ackee and Saltfish 162

79. Sorrel 164

80. Irish Moss 165

81. Carrot Juice 167

Martinique **168**

82. Accra 168

83. Boudin 170

84. Chatrou 172

85. Colombo 174

86. Lambis 176

87. Le Matautou de Crabe 178

88. Le Feroce d'Avocat 180

Montserrat **182**
    89. Goat Water 182
Netherlands **184**
    90. Pannenkoeken 184
    91. Erwtensoep 186
Puerto Rico **188**
    92. Mofongo 188
    93. Chicken Asopao 190
    94. Puerto Rican Roasted Pork 192
    95. Arroz con Pollo 194
Saint Barthelemy (St. Barths) **196**
    96. Feroce D'Avocat 196
    97. Mahi Mahi 198
St. Kitts and Nevis **200**
    98. Coconut Dumplings 200
    99. Seasoned Breadfruit 202
    100. Conch Salad 204
St. Lucia **205**
    101. Breadfruit Pie 205
    102. Greenfig Salad 207
St. Martin & St. Maarten **208**
    103. Rum Barbecue Sauce 208
    104. Jerked King Fish 210
St. Vincent & The Grenadines **211**
    105. Stuffed Sweet Potatoes 211
    106. Green Pigeon Peas Soup 213

Trinidad & Tobago 215
    107. Cow Heel Soup 215
    108. Curry Mango 217
    109. Baighan Chokha 219
    110. Pholourie 221
    111. Macaroni Pie 223
Turks & Caicos Islands 225
    112. Ginger Mango Chicken 225
    113. Fish Batter 227
US Virgin Islands 228
    114. Crab & Rice 228
    115. Stuffed Eggplant 230
Caribbean Tools & Utensils 232
Conclusion 233
Cooking Measurements & Conversions 234

Introduction

Welcome to the follow-up to my first book, (Most Popular Caribbean Recipes Quick and Easy). If you had enjoyed the first book, thank you. Due to the fantastic response that I had received, I wanted to shine a light on many more of the islands that contribute to the Caribbean's great cuisine.

Welcome to 115 Greatest Caribbean Recipes of All Time. These recipes are understood to be the greatest because they have remained popular throughout many years, amongst natives, expats and visitors alike. Recipes that are favorites of Islands whose foods are delicious and delectable, but are unlikely to receive the exposure that they deserve.

The good food stems from the melting pot of influences from all over the globe throughout history that culminate in the islands and as a result most people do not realise how varied the dishes are from Island to Island. African, European, British, Spanish, Portuguese and East Indian are just a few of the influences and flavor profiles you can expect to encounter as the variety of dishes and beverages grace your palate.

In this cookbook, you can expect to find 115 undeniably tasty recipes from 26 different islands within the Caribbean, each with its own historical background and unique taste. Only popular, well-known recipes, synonymous with each individual Island are represented here. Dishes that are sure to take you back to a time when you once visited, or to transport you to an Island that you may intend to visit. Recipes that capture the true essence of the whole Caribbean, from Islands such as Aruba, British Virgin Islands, Caymans, Curacao, Guadeloupe and Montserrat as well as the ever-popular islands of Cuba, Haiti, Jamaica, Trinidad, Barbados and many others.

To understand the recipes within, it's helpful to understand the history and influence of an Island's cuisine. Here is a food history of some of the featured islands.

Bahamas

Bahamian cuisine includes a lot of seafood, including lobster, crab and conch. The distinctive flavors offered by various dishes are said to resemble the flavors of the southern states of America. Another hallmark of Bahamian cuisine is the well-seasoned and spicy nature of many of the dishes. The sheer simplicity of the preparation of these dishes, makes the task of wowing your guests or recreating a favorite dish very easy.

Barbados

Barbadian or Bajan cuisine has been largely influenced by British, Indian, Irish, Creole and African cultures. The national dish Flying fish with Cou Cou is aptly so, especially since the flying fish is the most widely caught fish on the island. Barbados is also very popular for its rums.

Cayman Islands

There is a striking similarity between the flavors you will get coming out of Cayman and those from Jamaica. This is due to the use of Jamaican jerk seasoning on their meats and fish. There is also influence from other islands around the Caribbean, Britain and in recent times as well as America. You will commonly find that the traditional Caymanian meals make use of fish, turtle, conch and goat.

Cuba

When we think of Cuba we think of Spanish influence, so it comes as no surprise that Cuban cuisine has a heavy Spanish influence also. This was a result of colonization and was combined with Taino, Native American, African, French and Caribbean undertones as well. Much of the cuisine has also been influenced by the tropical climate enjoyed on the Island, which makes ground provisions and tropical fruit, a popular feature of Cuban meals. Not to be forgotten is the typical rice and beans or arroz y frijoles, the preparation of which may vary depending on where in Cuba you are visiting.

Curacao

The strong Dutch and Indonesian influence can be seen in common meals from Curacao as well as from the rest of the Caribbean region and Latin America. The same can be expected of the cuisine found in Bonaire and Aruba. The popular Stoba and the breakfast food Pastechi, are just two of the foods you can expect to find throughout Curacao, not excluding the local food shops.

Dominica

Interestingly, Dominican cuisine is strikingly similar to that which can be found in St. Lucia and Trinidad. The fusion of Caribbean, African, French and Asian cultures on Dominica's cuisine is very evident. Dominica is also popular for a very wide selection of tropical fruit juices owing to the broad range of tropical fruit that they produce locally.

Jamaica

True to their motto, "out of many, one people", Jamaica has incorporated into its cuisine, Spanish, British, African, Indian, Chinese and even Irish influences. Many of these were incorporated as a result of slavery and the cultures to which they were introduced during those times. Jamaican food is greatly renowned to be well seasoned and spicy, as is typical of the very sought after jerk chicken and curry goat. Many of their recipes make use of locally grown, ground provisions to fully utilize what is native to the country.

St. Lucia

St. Lucia is popularly known for its green fig salad which consists of green bananas and salt fish. The culinary influence left by the Arawaks and Caribs who occupied the island prior to slavery has now been combined with the British, French and East Indian influences post slavery. Lemon squash is a popular refreshment after a hearty St. Lucian meal.

Trinidad and Tobago

Trinidadian cuisine is known for its curries, which demonstrates the strong Indian influence. Along with this are influences from Amerindian, African, Creole, French, British and Spanish cultures. The various types of roti, pelau and the herb chadon beni are all synonymous with Trinidadian culture.

Similarities in Cuisine across the Region

From the few islands we've just looked at, it is clear that Caribbean cuisine is truly multicultural on a global scale. The amalgamation of different flavors spices, herbs, seasonings and cooking methods coupled with the use of locally available tropical foods makes Caribbean cuisine truly redolent of a mixed heritage.

In the Lesser Antilles of the Caribbean region, you will find that some dishes overlap, as they have shared similar occupation of various nationalities in colonial times. The peleau in Trinidad, Grenada and St.Vincent, is known as 'cook up' in Guyana. This is purely based on the language influence. Cow heels soup in Trinidad is cow foot soup in Jamaica. In fact rice and peas in Jamaica is known all across the region as peas and rice.

Another similarity to be found across the islands is the use of codfish or saltfish. Although cod is mostly an imported fish, the proximity to the sea of the islands makes fish in itself a popular meal option, prepared in so many different ways.

Even with the similarities in the cuisine of the Caribbean Sea, there are beautiful variations to the preparation of certain dishes and beverages, which are only to be embraced. Each Island may champion its way of doing things as, 'the way' but it is in our differences that we are able to see other perspectives and appreciate that another method is also quite acceptable. A case in point can be seen in the meal macaroni pie. Classic macaroni pie stays true to being simply macaroni with lots of cheese. In fact, some would argue that the correct term is macaroni and cheese. That aside you will find that Bajan macaroni pie includes ketchup, an addition that many would not have thought of.

The Caribbean connection can further be seen between Montserrat and Jamaica for example, goat water in Montserrat is Manish water in Jamaica. Both give very different ideas of what exactly this dish proposes to be. The unifying element is the use of goat meat, which is neither watery nor 'manish', but is a hearty and rich goat meat soup and also a comfort food.

Please journey with us now as we go island hopping from one delectable delight to the next. Your palate will be excited as you experience the flavors and aromas of each dish. The ingredients are not difficult to source so just go right ahead as you chef up these Caribbean creations form the comfort of your kitchen. Now transport yourself to the Caribbean, simply choose your Island of interest, select a recipe and head over to food paradise…sunshine and good food awaits!

FREE Bonuses

We have 3 **FREE** bonus cookbooks for your enjoyment!

- **Cookie Cookbook** 2134 recipes
- **Cake Cookbook** 2444 recipes
- **Mac and Cheese Cookbook** 103 recipes

Simply visit: **www.ffdrecipes.com** to get your **FREE** recipe ebooks.

You will also receive free exclusive access to our World Recipes Club, giving you FREE best-selling book offers, discounts and recipe ideas, delivered to your inbox regularly.

Anguilla

1. Anguillan Chicken Sausage

This delectable chicken sausage consists of a fusion of actual chorizo sausage with crayfish and chicken, all enveloped in a layer of chicken as the casing. The combination produces an exquisite flavor to tantalize the taste buds with a zing of ginger.

Serves 1

Ingredients

2 oz chicken breast
4 oz flattened chicken breast
2 oz crayfish flesh
1 ½ oz ground chorizo sausage
1 oz julienned ginger
1 oz julienned leeks
1 oz heavy cream
2 minced garlic cloves
1 oz chopped onions
1 tsp chopped fresh cilantro
1 oz sesame oil
Salt and pepper to taste

Preparation

1. Add all the vegetables except the ginger, to a medium sauce pan and sauté with the sesame oil.

2. After two minutes add the chorizo sausage and crayfish, also add salt and pepper to taste.
3. Remove from heat and let the mixture cool. Chill in the refrigerator.
4. Place the two ounces of chicken breast and the cream into a food processor. Process until they form a paste.
5. Mix the paste, crayfish and vegetables and cilantro together. Add more salt and pepper if desired.
6. Season the flattened chicken breast with salt and pepper then add some of the crayfish/sausage/chicken mixture with a spoon. Use plastic wrap to roll it closed.
7. Braise the chicken breast until it just becomes golden brown. Cook until just right and serve while still hot.

Pairs well with - Rice, mashed potatoes, steamed vegetables

2. Crispy Lobster and Vegetable Spring Roll with Soya Lobster Dressing

This delicious spring roll from Anguilla makes the perfect starter to any meal. Make it even more interesting with various dipping sauces and experiment with the flavors.

Serves 4

Ingredients

2 julienned leeks
4 julienned carrots
5 oz snow peas
6 sheets filo dough
2, 5 oz lobster tails (in the shells)
Lobster oil
Roasted sesame seeds
Soy sauce
Ground black pepper
Chopped chives
Mixed green salad

For Dressing
Mustard
Red wine vinegar
Soy sauce
Tabasco sauce

Preparation

1. Julienne all the vegetables (including the ones from the green salad) and sauté in a little of the lobster oil.
2. Add chives, some sesame seeds and black pepper. Set aside.
3. Boil the lobster tails in water with salt and black pepper added, for about 8 minutes.
4. Shred the lobster tails and add the meat to the sautéed vegetables prepared earlier. Mix them together well.
5. Lay a sheet of the filo dough on the counter, brush with lobster and add another sheet on top.
6. Spoon the lobster mixture on the dough and roll to seal.
7. Cut the roll into 8 equal pieces, brush the tops with lobster oil and sprinkle with sesame seeds.
8. Bake in an oven which was preheated to 400 °F for 10 minutes.

To Make the Dressing

1. Combine some mustard, red wine vinegar, soy sauce, a few drops of Tabasco sauce along with some lobster oil and mix well.
2. Use as dip with the spring rolls.

Pairs well with - citrus chilli sauce

3. Grilled Chicken Parts with Barbecue Sauce

Enjoy this tasty grilled chicken with an amplified flavor of roasted pine nuts and the sweetness of mango chutney for a tropical flair.

Serves 4

Ingredients

3 tsp olive oil
1 chopped garlic clove
1 chopped medium onion
1 chopped bell pepper (red or green)
3 peeled and chopped medium tomatoes
8 oz water
6 tsp mango chutney
¼ cup roasted ground pine nuts
1 tsp thyme
2 oz hot pepper sauce
1 chicken (medium sized) cut into 8 (2 pieces each of leg, breast, thigh and wing)

Preparation

1. In a large saucepan sauté the chopped onions in olive oil for two minutes, then add the garlic and sauté for a further five minutes.
2. Add the bell peppers and sauté for five minutes more.
3. Add the tomatoes then sauté for five minutes. Cover the saucepan and leave to cook for an additional twenty minutes.

4. Add all the other ingredients, except the chicken and allow them to simmer for five minutes. Remove and puree in a blender or food processor then set aside.
5. On a grill, smoke the chicken parts until they are cooked halfway.
6. Use a brush to coat the parts on both sides and continue to smoke grill them until they are fully cooked.

Pairs well with – White rice, rice and peas or mashed potatoes

4. Lemon Herb Butter

This tangy blend of lemon and herbs is great for fish dishes and also as an accompaniment for shellfish.

Ingredients

1 lb butter
3 teaspoons lemon juice
1 teaspoon dill
1 teaspoon powdered garlic

Preparation
1. Allow butter reach room temperature to soften.
2. Mix all the ingredients together with the butter and store in the refrigerator.

Pairs well with – Snapper, pasta

5. Lobster Cakes with Tartar Sauce

Tangy sauces pair very well with seafood dishes and these lobster cakes go seamlessly with this tomato tartar sauce.

Serves 10 (if each person gets 3, 2 inch cakes)

Ingredients

3 tbsp unsalted butter
¾ cup flour
16 oz milk
1lb cooked lobster meat (dried and chopped coarsely)
1 ½ cups diced and dried red bell pepper
¼ cup thinly sliced scallions
½ tsp cayenne pepper
¾ tsp salt
½ tsp ground black pepper
1 ½ cups bread crumbs
50:50 butter and olive oil to sauté

Tomato Tartar Sauce

1 cup Mayonnaise
3 teaspoons fresh lemon juice
3 teaspoons tomato paste
6 teaspoons minced onion
3 teaspoons capers (rinsed and drained)
¼ cup dill pickles (minced and patted dry)
Salt and ground black pepper to taste

Preparation

For cakes

1. Heat the butter in a deep saucepan. When the butter stops foaming, add the flour a small amount at a time, whisking continuously.
2. Add a quarter of the milk at a time, whisking continuously with each addition to avoid lumps.
3. Allow to simmer for five minutes while whisking. Turn off and remove from heat when smooth and thick.
4. Mix the lobster, bell peppers, scallions, cayenne pepper, black pepper and salt together.
5. Add the mixture you had set aside along with 2/3 of the breadcrumbs and combine well. Allow to cool to room temperature.
6. Shape the cakes into 1 to 2 inch wide cakes which are about a half an inch thick. Make them slightly flat. Dip into bread crumbs to coat them evenly.
7. Heat some of the butter and oil mixture in a frying pan over a medium flame until just hot.
8. Fry the cakes to golden brown in both sides. Drain excess oil on paper towels before serving.

For Sauce

Combine well the mayonnaise, tomato paste and lemon juice, then mix in the remaining ingredients.

Pairs well with – Regular tartar sauce and mixed green salad

6. Lobster Pancakes

A perfect start to your fancy dinner party, these lobster pancakes will be a hit. The creamy tangy sauce adds to the perfection and the colorful garnish adds various textures and visual appeal for a stunning presentation.

Serves 4

Ingredients

1 lb sweet potatoes
6 teaspoons butter
1 egg
4 oz milk
1 tsp baking powder
½ cup flour
½ tsp grated nutmeg
Salt and black pepper to taste
Two lobster tails (between 8 and 10 oz)

For Sauce

1 Cup dry white wine
3 teaspoons fresh lemon juice
2 oz tarragon vinegar
4 minced shallots
½ teaspoon peppercorns
1 pint heavy cream (for whipping)
2 sprigs fresh parsley

For Garnish

2 peeled sweet potatoes
1 ½ cup peanut oil
1 sliced red onion
6 teaspoons unsalted butter
6 teaspoons balsamic vinegar
2 oz lobster roe
2 tomatoes (peeled, seeds removed, diced)
8 sprigs thyme (or 4 sprigs stingy thyme)

Preparation

Preparing the lobster:

1. Place a medium saucepan to which water and salt has been added on high heat. Allow to boil.
2. Cook the tails in the water for between five and six minutes.
3. Remove with tongs and immediately immerse in ice cold water to stop cooking.
4. Carefully crack the shells and remove the meat in whole pieces. Slice each tail thinly into rounds (medallions) and set aside for later use.

For the pancakes:

1. Set oven to 350 °F beforehand.
2. Sprinkle a little salt and pepper on each potato, add a pat of butter and wrap individually in foil.

3. Bake for one hour or until they become soft.
4. Peel potatoes and crush them in a bowl.
5. Place the potatoes along with the egg and milk into a food processor. Blend until smooth.
6. Into the food processor, add the flour, nutmeg and baking powder. Process again until smooth. Mixture can be thickened with more flour or thinned with some milk. Consistency should be for pouring. Add a little salt and pepper to taste.
7. On a medium-high flame, place a frying pan and lightly cover with oil.
8. Pour the batter into the pan, three circles at a time, about 3 inches wide for each.
9. When the tops begin to bubble, place a lobster round on top of each and gently flip over. Remove them after about two minutes or when golden brown.
10. Place onto a heated plate and store in a warm oven until ready to serve.

For the sauce:

1. Add all ingredients and mix together, excluding the cream, into a large sauce pan with a thick bottom.
2. Allow it to simmer and reduce until about a third of the mixture remains.
3. Add the cream, simmer for 10-15 minutes then strain.

For the garnish:

1. Using any style of slicer you prefer, shred the peeled sweet potatoes into thin strips and dry with a towel.
2. In a large sauce pan, heat the oil then put a quarter of the strips in when the oil begins to ripple.
3. When they rise to the surface, remove the strips and drain using a paper towel. Repeat with the remaining strips.
4. Slice the onion into rings and sauté them in melted butter on a medium-high flame until they become brown. Drain on a paper towel.
5. Place in a bowl and toss them with balsamic vinegar. Leave to stand.

To serve the pancakes:

1. Place some lobster roe around the edges of the serving plates then arrange some stingy thyme leaves in the centre.
2. Add some of the sauce b over the thyme leaves then add some diced tomatoes
3. Arrange three of the pancakes in a circular manner, with each slightly overlapping the other.
4. Top the cakes with the onion rings, then add the fried sweet potatoes on top of that. Finish with a single thyme leaf topper.

Pairs well with – maple syrup

7. Stuffed Chicken Breast

The tenderness of this entree coupled with the softness of the mushrooms, onions and tomatoes on the inside make for an interesting combination. A third element of delight is the nutty crunch afforded by the almonds and walnuts.

Serves 1

Ingredients

5 oz chicken breast
1 oz chicken (diced)
Butter
2 oz tomatoes (diced)
Mushrooms
Green onions
Spinach leaves (poached)
1 egg
Flour
Salt and pepper
Sliced almonds
Crushed walnuts

Preparation

1. Sauté the diced chicken, mushrooms, onions and tomatoes in a little butter.
2. Remove from the heat, then add the egg on top as well as pepper and salt. Allow to cool.

3. Flatten the chicken breast and lightly season with salt and pepper.
4. Add a layer of the spinach leaves on the breast then add the cooled stuffing.
5. Roll the chicken breast then coat with the almonds and walnuts mixed together.
6. Bake it in an oven set to 400 °F for not more than 15 minutes.

Pairs well with - Light mushroom sauce, mashed potatoes, pasta

8. Warm Chocolate Pie

This warm, delectable, pudding-like dessert gives the perfect end to a wonderful meal – and we all aware that chocolate is comfort food.

Serves 6 to 8

Ingredients

2 oz butter
2 oz sugar
1 egg yolk
1 loaf white bread (crumbs)
2 oz melted dark chocolate
1 egg white (whipped)
2 oz mixed nuts

Preparation

1. Preheat oven to 350 °F.
2. Beat butter, sugar and egg yolk with a mixer until creamy.
3. Add in the bread crumbs as well as the melted chocolate and mix well.
4. Fold in the whipped egg white followed by the mixed nuts.
5. Pour into greased and floured pan then bake until done.

Pairs well with - warm vanilla sauce and fresh berries

Antigua and Barbuda

9. Black Angel Hair Fritters

A seafood appetizer with a difference, these fritters combine crab and conch to make an interesting mix, all brought together by pasta.

Serves 2

Ingredients

2 oz Blue crab meat
2 oz conch (minced)
2 oz vegetables (minced)
1 oz black angel hair pasta (cooked)
1 egg
Baking powder
Black pepper and salt

Preparation

1. Combine crab meat and conch then add the minced vegetables, egg and a small amount of baking powder. Mix well.
2. Add salt and pepper to taste then carefully add the angel hair pasta.

3. In a deep fryer heated to 250 °F, add a portion of the mixture and remove when fried. Continue until all the fritters are fried.

Pairs well with – mild curry sauce and diced tomatoes

10. Conch Fritters

Experience the distinctive flavor of celery along with the spicy kick of jerk sauce in these lovely conch fritters.

Serves 8

Ingredients

1 lb cooked conch (chopped)
2 celery stalks
2 beaten eggs
1 cup flour
4 garlic cloves
1 teaspoon baking powder
1 green bell pepper (seeds removed)
1 teaspoon salt
1 white onion
2 oz milk
1 carrot
6 teaspoons jerk sauce

Preparation

1. Process the conch little by little in a food processor.
2. Place into a large bowl and mix in the eggs.
3. Put the garlic, green pepper, onion, carrot and celery into the food processor until they are finely chopped.

4. Drain them through a sieve lined with cheese cloth to remove the excess water then add them to the conch in the bowl and stir.
5. Combine the baking powder and flour then mix with other ingredients.
6. Add the milk, salt and finally the jerk sauce, folding them into the mixture to make a dough. Cover and place it into the fridge for no less than an hour.
7. Set a deep fryer to 400 °F. Remove the dough from the refrigerator and let it sit for about 20 minutes.
8. Use a tablespoon to drop the fritters into the oil and fry them until golden brown.
9. Allow the fritters to drain on a paper towel and serve while still hot.

Pairs well with - Caribbean Tartar Sauce

11. Ducuna

This pudding-like dish serves as a dessert and is called Dukunu or tie a leaf in Jamaica. The recipe is also slightly different with the addition of coconut and possibly cornmeal. Other islands such as St. Vincent, Barbados and Trinidad also have their own variations.

Serves 5

Ingredients

2 large sweet potatoes
½ cup sugar
2 ½ cups flour
All spice
Cinnamon
Raisins

Preparation

1. Grate the sweet potatoes and add sugar to them. Allow the mixture to sit to produce water.
2. Add the flour as well as the spices and raisins. (If the mixture seems too thick, add water, if it is too watery, some flour).

3. Use a spoon to place some of the mixture onto foil paper. Wrap it in a rectangular shape and put in a pot with boiling water for 45 minutes. It is firm when finished and can be had while still hot.

Pairs well with - saltfish

12. Papaya Pie

Similar to peach or apricot pies, this papaya pie stays true to the tropics, making use of what is locally available. It's simple to make and you can add extra spice by including nutmeg and allspice.

Serves 6 to 8

Ingredients

1 Medium sized pre-baked pie sweet pie crust
3 Ripe papayas (medium-sized)
2 teaspoons lime juice
½ teaspoon lime zest
Cinnamon
Orange extract
¼ cup flour
¼ cup sugar
4 beaten egg whites

Preparation

1. Remove the papaya seeds and roughly crush them.
2. Add the lime juice, lime zest, a dash of cinnamon and orange extract to the papayas and mix lightly.
3. Add the flour and sugar then fold in the beaten egg whites.

4. Spoon into pie crust and bake at 400 °F for 25 minutes until the top becomes slightly brown.
5. Chill and serve.

Pairs well with – Vanilla ice cream or whipped cream

13. Pineapple Trifle

This textured dessert will allow you to enjoy the best of both worlds without feeling too guilty. The cake and fruit together with a kick of alcohol will delight the palate.

Serves 24 people

Ingredients

2 cup butter
2 cup sugar
2 medium cans crushed pineapple
1 small jar of cherries (minced, keep juice)
8 eggs, separated
Vanilla
Rum
Large plain sheet cake

Preparation

1. Beat the butter and sugar together in a large bowl, adding the sugar a little at a time.
2. Pour the water off from the pineapples and keep, then mix the crushed pineapples, cherries and egg yolks into the sugar and butter mixture.

3. Beat the egg whites until peaks form then fold it into the mixture.
4. Make a syrup with the pineapple juice, cherry juice, vanilla and rum.
5. Slice the plain cake into three layers with a knife moistened with the syrup.
6. Spread the creamed mixture on the first layer then sprinkle with syrup.
7. Add the second layer, then repeat and finally the third layer on top.
8. Top the final layer also with syrup then the remainder of the cream. Pineapple and cherry pieces may be added as garnish.

Pairs well with – whipped cream

14. Pork Chops with Banana and Bacon

This combination of pork with bacon and potatoes may sound like an unlikely pairing. The result is a beautiful marriage of flavors, that gets even more interesting when you add the beer.

Serves 4

Ingredients

4 1 inch thick pork chops
2 ¼ tsps cumin
Salt and black pepper
Juice from 1 lemon
6 tsps softened butter
2 large ripe bananas
6 bacon strips
Beer (if desired)

Preparation

1. Mix the butter, salt, pepper and cumin together and rub on both sides of the pork chops.
2. Place the bacon in a hot frying pan until some of the oil just starts to come off. Remove from pan and drain.
3. Peel the ripe bananas and cut them into 1 ¼ inch rounds then put them in a dish and drizzle with lemon juice.

4. Slice the bacon strips lengthwise, long enough so that they can wrap completely around each piece of banana.
5. Put the banana bacon wrap on skewers, piercing where the bacon overlaps.
6. Heat up a grill and put the pork chops on it for 15 minutes on each side.
7. Reduce the flame on the grill to a medium setting then add the bacon bananas for 10 minutes, while the chops are still on. Turn both once during this time. Add beer at this point if desired.

Pairs well with – herbed rice, rice and peas or baked potatoes

Aruba

15. Bolita di Keshi

These cheese balls are ideal to be served as a meal starter or a snack. To experience the authentic Dutch Caribbean flavors of Aruba, try mixing the sharp cheddar with some Edam or Gouda cheese.

Serves 9 to 12 (yields 36 cheese balls)

Ingredients

1 lb sharp grated cheddar
2 eggs
1 tsp baking powder
2 cup Flour
Garlic powder
Cooking oil

Preparation

1. Combine all the ingredients together in a bowl except the oil.
2. Knead into a dough then cover with a damp cloth for at least one hour.
3. Shape the dough into little balls and deep fry in hot oil until they are golden brown.

4. Drain on paper towels then serve while still hot. Use toothpicks.

Pairs well with – honey mustard sauce

16. Arepa

These small loaves are an ideal substitute for bread especially at breakfast time. They are very quick and easy to make and also come in handy as a snack during the day.

Serves 4

Ingredients

1 tsp salt
1 cup White corn flour (pre-cooked)
10 oz warm water

Preparation

1. Add the salt to the water then pour a small amount at a time to the corn flour in a mixing bowl. Mix to form a dough. Leave for 5 minutes.
2. Form the dough into round 3 inch balls about ½ inch thick.
3. Lightly grease a pan and allow the balls to cook slowly until they form a crust on either side.

4. Preheat the oven to 350 °F and put the balls in a baking dish and bake for about twenty minutes. To ensure the arepas are ready, a hollow sound should be heard when you tap them.

Note: Broth may be substituted for plain water.

Pairs well with – butter, grated cheese, scrambled eggs, black beans

17. Balchi di Pisca

These tasty fish balls can alternatively be made using salmon or other types of fish fillets instead of the salted codfish.

Serves 3

Ingredients

1 salted codfish
3 peeled medium-sized potatoes (diced)
1 tomato (skin removed and chopped)
½ green bell pepper (chopped)
1 medium-sized onion (chopped)
1 garlic clove (sliced lengthwise)
½ teaspoon Tabasco sauce
Grated nutmeg
Salt and pepper
1 egg

Preparation

1. Soak the codfish for 24 hours.
2. Cover the codfish with water in a saucepan then gently simmer until the fish can be easily flaked with a fork.
3. Strain the liquid off and reserve a small amount. Remove the bones form the fish and set aside.
4. Boil the potatoes until tender then drain.
5. Crush the codfish with the potatoes and set aside.

6. Put the tomatoes, green peppers, onion, garlic, Tabasco sauce, some nutmeg and salt and pepper in a blender for a couple of seconds.
7. Pour the blended mixture over the codfish and potatoes then add the beaten egg.
8. Form them into 1 ½ inch balls and fry them in hot oil until golden brown.

    Note: If the mixture is too dry, add the broth that was retained one tablespoon each time.

Pairs well with – tutu, potatoes or rice

18. Banana den Forno

This sweet treat is meant to be had as a snack but it can easily be converted into an after-dinner dessert by adding your favorite flavor of ice cream.

Serves 4

Ingredients

4 ripe bananas
6 tsps cinnamon powder
9 tsps vanilla
1 cup Sugar
2 pints water

Preparation

1. Remove the banana peels then boil the bananas with cinnamon, vanilla, sugar and water for twenty minutes.

2. Preheat the oven to 275 °F.

3. Bake the bananas for ten minutes.

Pairs well with – Ice cream

19. Bitterbal (Meat Croquettes)

These meat-filled balls were originally made from left over dinner meats and served as fillers in between lunch and dinner.

Serves 3

Ingredients

3 tbsp butter
3 tbsp flour
6 oz stock
1 ½ cup minced pre-cooked meat (of your choosing)
1 tbsp minced parsley
Salt and pepper
Crushed cracker crumbs
1 beaten egg
2 tbsp water

Preparation

1. Make a roux by adding the butter to a sauce pan, then the flour then the stock. Turn off when it becomes thickened.
2. Add the meat, parsley, and salt and pepper.
3. Chill the mixture then make balls about one inch thick.
4. Roll the balls in the cracker crumbs, then egg, then water and once again into the crumbs.
5. Fry the balls preferably in a deep fryer until they are golden brown.

Pairs well with – hot mustard or fries

Bahamas

20. Bahama Papa

You will find that this cocktail drink recipe has quite a number of variations for alcoholic additives. What is common to all is the inclusion of pineapple juice. This is definitely the manlier counterpart of the Bahama Mama.

Serves 1

Ingredients

1 ¼ oz Captain Morgan's rum
2 oz Red Grapefruit Juice
1 oz pineapple juice
¾ oz Dark Rum
Orange wedge to garnish
Cherry with pit removed to garnish

Preparation

1. Pour all the ingredients together in a spindle mixer.

2. Pour over ice into a glass of your choice.

3. Garnish and serve.

Pairs well with – Cocktail of your choice, nuts

21. Sky Juice

The Sky Juice dates all the way back to the early twentieth century. Canned juices and sodas were not then readily accessible so the local people made use of coconut water and other available tropical fruit juices. The authentic Sky Juice of the Bahamas always includes gin which was very affordable even at that time. As a result, this drink became very popular in bars, and still is a favorite of Bahamian natives and visitors.

Serves 1

Ingredients

6 oz Coconut Water
2 oz Gin
1 oz Condensed Milk
Ground Nutmeg

Preparation

1. Put the coconut water, gin, and milk together into a cocktail shaker. Shake vigorously to combine.
2. Pour the contents into a cocktail glass with ice then sprinkle a bit of the nutmeg to add flavor.

Pairs well with – Rice and Peas, Macaroni and cheese, Conch, Fried fish

22. Goombay Smash

This potent creation is definitely not for the weak willed with its blend of four rums. It is actually Bahamas' national drink and was so named for the traditional Bahamian drumming music which is akin to calypso.

Serves 2

Ingredients

6 tbsp pineapple juice
¼ cup orange juice
¼ cup coconut rum
2 tbsp light rum
2 tbsp gold rum
2 tbsp dark rum
2 pineapple wedges
2 orange slices

Preparation

1. In a cocktail shaker filled with ice pour the pineapple and orange juice, as well as all the rums.
2. Cover the container and shake it until it becomes very cold.
3. Add ice to 2 short glasses and strain while pouring equal amounts in each.
4. Garnish each glass with an orange slice and a pineapple wedge.

Pairs well with – any meal

23. Lionfish Tacos

With the invasion of the lionfish into Caribbean waters a few years ago, recipes containing the fish gradually increased in popularity. The texture of this fish makes it a choice option for breakfast, lunch or dinner and these tasty tacos prove that. This spicy and tangy creation packs huge flavor.

Serves 4

Ingredients

1lb lionfish fillets (8 of them)
Oil to deep fry
2 limes
4 ¼ oz flour
8 6 inch tortillas
¼ cabbage (shredded)
½ bell pepper (red, julienned)
1 bell pepper (green, julienned)
1 goat pepper (minced)
2 garlic cloves (minced)
½ cup cilantro (freshly picked, chopped)
½ cup sour cream

Preparation

1. Preheat the oil in the deep fryer to 350 °F.
2. Marinate the fillets in a lime juice, salt, and pepper mixture.
3. Dip the fillets in flour to coat.

4. Fry until they become golden brown.
5. Combine the cabbage, peppers, garlic, cilantro and sour cream.
6. Add salt and pepper as desired.
7. Add a fillet to a tortilla and top with some of the cabbage mixture. Repeat with other tortillas and serve with lime wedges if preferred.

Pairs well with – fries or lettuce and tomatoes

Barbados

24. Cou cou

Cou cou along with flying fish constitutes Barbados' national dish. With a similar consistency to polenta and grits, Cou cou is a delightful mix of cornmeal with okra.

Serves 4

Ingredients

8 oz cornmeal
3 oz okras
1 chopped medium onion
3 tbsp butter
Water
Salt as desired

Preparation

1. Add enough water to cover the cornmeal in a bowl and leave to soak.
2. Cut the stems and tips of the okras then slice making rings.
3. Put them in a saucepan along with onions, salt and boil on medium heat for a little while to soften.
4. Strain and retain liquid.

5. Place a quarter of the liquid and the soaked cornmeal into the saucepan on a medium flame and stir with a wooden spoon while cooking to prevent lumps.
6. Add more liquid little by little until the mixture starts to gently bubble.
7. Add the okras and continue to stir for a further 2 to 3 minutes.
8. Turn off flame then add in butter and serve.

Pairs well with - Gravy and flying fish

25. Flying Fish

Quite a popular Bajan dish Flying fish will go hand in hand with Cou cou. This twice coated recipe makes for a tender and juicy fried fish with a heavenly crust.

Serves 5 to 10

Ingredients

10 flying fish cutlets
2 limes
2 tbsp Salt
1 ½ cups Water
3 tbsp <u>Bajan seasoning</u>
2 cup seasoned breadcrumbs
1 cup Flour
3 Eggs, beaten with pepper and salt
Canola Oil for frying

Preparation

1. Place the juice of the limes, the squeezed limes, salt and water together in a bowl with the fish and rest for 10 to 15 minutes, covered.

2. Rinse fish with a little water, drain and dry then coat with the <u>Bajan Seasoning</u>.

3. Put the oil to heat in a frying pan.

4. Dip the seasoned fish first into the flour, then the eggs, then the bread crumbs then fry. Repeat with the others until finished.

Pairs well with – Cou cou, fries, green salad, rice and peas, macaroni pie

26. Salt Bread

Most Bajan breads are sweet so this recipe is one of the few savoury types of bread you will find in Barbados. They are made into large rolls which can be sliced prior to using.

Ingredients

6 ½ cup White flour
2 tsps granulated sugar
1 tsp salt
2 tbsp vegetable oil
2 packs dried active yeast
18 oz warm water

Preparation

1. Mix in a large bowl half of the sifted flour with the salt and yeast.

2. Add the warm water slowly with continuous mixing to form a firm dough which you can knead.

3. Use a floured surface to knead the dough for approx 10 minutes. It will get smoother and become elastic.

4. Put the dough into a greased bowl and stow in a warm area for up to 50 minutes.

5. Set oven to 425 °F.

6. Remove the dough and form into 12 equal fist sized balls.

7. Place them on a greased baking tray then leave in a warm place for another 40 minutes.

8. Bake on the middle rack of oven for twenty-five minutes to half an hour. Rolls should sound hollow when they are tapped to indicate readiness.

Pairs well with – butter, sandwich fillers

27. Cutters

A Barbados cutter is an assemblage of freshly made Bajan salt bread with a savoury filling of your choice. They are commonly had at lunch but can be consumed at any time of the day. Common fillings are fish, ham, cheese, liver or eggs, with lettuce and tomatoes added. A spicy kick is what you can expect from this fish cutter recipe which boasts Bajan hot sauce and jerk spice.

Serves 4

Ingredients

4 Lettuce Leaves
1 cup Flour
1 Beefy Tomato
3 tsps powdered jerk Spice
1 bottle Bajan hot sauce
4 Fillets White Fish
4 Cheddar Cheese Slices
2 White Bread Slices
2 Eggs

For the Bread

3 cups White Flour
2 tbsp Butter
3 tbsp Granulated Sugar
1 tsp Salt
1 tsp Active Dry Yeast
1 cup warm water

Preparation

To make the bread

1. Combine the flour, salt and butter together until the mix becomes crumby.
2. Add the yeast and sugar to the warm water and rest for 1 minute then add to the crumb mixture a little at a time.
3. Knead on a floured surface for about 10 minutes then cover and leave for about 40 minutes to rise.
4. Punch the dough then remove and divide into six portions.
5. Make 6 balls then place them on a baking sheet and rest for half an hour.
6. Brush them with water then bake at 425 °F for fifteen to twenty minutes.

Preparing the fish

1. Make breadcrumbs from the white bread slices in a bowl and stir in the jerk spice.
2. Beat the eggs in a separate bowl.
3. Coat each fillet first with flour then egg then breadcrumbs.
4. In a frying pan on high heat, add some oil to cover the bottom and fry each fillet. Drain on a paper towel.

To assemble

1. Slice one roll into two halves then add tomato, lettuce, fish then cheese on one half.

2. Top with hot sauce then cover with second half of roll. Follow suit for the other three rolls.

Pairs well with – fries, potato wedges, macaroni pie

28. Fish Cakes

Fish cakes are a consistent offering on most Bajan menus. They are light and airy ball shaped cakes which just melt in your mouth. Bursting with flavor, they are quite easy to make and you can recreate the ones you may have had before with the help of this simple recipe.

Serves 4
Ingredients

2 tbsp oil
1 cup onions, minced
1 cup flour
1 tsp baking powder
Salt
1 egg, beaten
6 oz milk
1 tbsp melted butter
2 tbsp Bajan Seasoning
½ lb salted cod fish (pre-cooked and flaked)
1 large minced hot pepper

Preparation

1. Sauté the onions in a hot frying pan until just tender.
2. Combine the flour, baking powder and salt in a container making a hole in the middle.
3. Add in the egg, milk and butter and lightly mix.
4. Stir in the onions, Bajan Seasoning, cod fish, salt and pepper.
5. Use a tablespoon to drop in dollops into the oil. Space them well.

Pairs well with – Marie-rose sauce, salt bread

British Virgin Islands

29. Baked Crab

This quick easy and delicious recipe can easily be substituted with lobster meat for another variation. The result is a lovely breaded crab cake with just the amount of spice you desire. You can make things more interesting by choosing a dipping sauce which has sweetness to it.

Serves 6

Ingredients

1 lb crab meat, cooked
2 eggs
4 tbsp melted butter
Bread crumbs
Salt and pepper to taste
Hot pepper sauce as desired
Oil for frying

Preparation

1. Combine the crab meat, butter, eggs and spices together.
2. Form the mixture into flattened cakes and coat with bread crumbs.
3. Fry on either side until they are golden brown.

Pairs well with – pasta salad, shrimp sauce, habanero sauce

30. Garlic Pork

If you are a lover of garlic then this recipe will certainly hit the spot for you. It also has a pickled flair since it is steeped in vinegar so there is a nice balance of heat, tanginess and garlic flavor.

Serves 6

Ingredients

3 or 4 lb lean pork (minimal fat)
2 pts vinegar
½ lb garlic cloves
1 bunch fresh thyme (mixed variety)
6 to 8 wiri wiri (cherry) peppers
4 to 6 whole cloves
4 tsps salt

Preparation

1. Cut up the pork and steep the pieces in a mixture of water and quarter of the vinegar portion (2 to 4 hours).
2. Remove the pork using two forks then place it into a large jar.
3. Beat the garlic with the peppers and thyme then add them to the remaining portion of vinegar.
4. Now add the salt and cloves to this mixture and finally pour it in the jar to cover all the pieces. Leave out for three or four days.

5. Place some of the pork into a sauce pan along with some of the seasoned liquid to boil until evaporation.
6. Allow the fat from the pork to fry the pieces until they become brown.

Pairs well with – bed of lettuce leaves, mashed potatoes

31. Lobster Salad

This super simple lobster salad is so quick to whip up and can be an effortless addition to your dinner menu. It has a kaleidoscope of flavors which are guaranteed to wow your taste buds as well as those of your guests.

Serves: 6

Ingredients

2 tbsp fresh lime or lemon juice
½ cup mayonnaise
12 oz cooked lobster (cut into ½" pieces)
¼ cup cucumber, diced
¼ cup onion, chopped
¼ cup celery, chopped
¼ cup green bell pepper, chopped
Salt and pepper
Hot pepper sauce

Preparation

1. Mix the lime or lemon juice and mayonnaise together.
2. Add in all the remaining ingredients and combine well.

Chill before serving.

Pairs well with – Green salad

32. Meat Pate

This meat pate bears some similarity to Jamaican patties, however this crust is not as flaky. It has a doughy consistency and the ground beef filling is deliciously well seasoned.

Serves 8

Ingredients

For Dough
5 cup flour
¼ c. vegetable shortening
2 tbsp baking powder
2 to 4 oz water

For Filling

½ lb lean ground beef
½ small onion (chopped)
1 small stick celery (chopped)
¼ tsp salt
2 tbsp green bell pepper(chopped)
Dried oregano
Black pepper
1 tsp kitchen bouquet (or browning)
2 tsps tomato paste
Parsley flakes
Garlic powder
 Small chopped hot pepper, to taste

Preparation

For dough

1. Put the flour, shortening, and baking powder all together into a mixing bowl.
2. Add water to form a dough and knead for not more than 15 minutes. Rest dough for 20 minutes.

For filling

1. In a large enough frying pan add all the filling ingredients in turn and cook them well. Vegetables should be softened and beef tender. Stir throughout cooking.
2. Strain off the excess fat using a strainer.
3. Split the dough into eight portions and roll them flat.
4. Spoon a tablespoon and a half of the beef mixture onto each, in the centre.
5. Fold over dough and seal the edges by pressing with a fork.
6. Deep fry the pates in oil heated to 360 °F until they are golden brown.

Pairs well with – any cold beverage or on their own

33. Okra Fungi

Fungi (pronounced as foon-jee), is a part of traditional British Virgin Islands cuisine. This cornmeal based dish is reminiscent of polenta but with okra added.

Serves 8

Ingredients

10 oz cut up okra
20 oz boiling water
1½ cup fine cornmeal
2 tbsp butter
¼ tsp salt and pepper

Preparation

1. Boil the okras until they are just tender.
2. Using the 20 ounces of water, bring it to a boil then add in a quarter cup of the cornmeal mixed into 6 ounces of water.
3. Add the remaining dry cornmeal slowly with constant stirring.
4. Add the cooked okra, butter and salt and pepper and mix well.
5. Allow to simmer for 5 minutes.

Pairs well with - boiled West Indian style fish or salt fish.

34. Rasta Pasta

The claim to fame of this pasta is its exciting and colorful appearance. The red, green and gold associated with Rastafarianism is captured by the yellow and red peppers as well as the green broccoli flowerets. This cheesy pasta pleases the palate as much as it pleases the eyes.

Serves 6 to 8

Ingredients

3 tbsp olive oil for frying
2 minced garlic cloves
1 large sliced onion
2 yellow and red peppers (deseeded and julienned)
1 lb fettuccini
1 tbsp olive oil for tossing with pasta
2 cup cooked black beans
2 cup cooked broccoli flowerets
¼ cup fresh basil (chopped)
2 tsps fresh oregano (chopped)
Grated parmesan cheese

Preparation

1. Sauté all the vegetables in the olive oil in a large frying pan until they are just tender.
2. Add the black beans.
3. Cook the fettuccini in boiling water with salt added.
4. Drain the water away then toss with the olive oil.

5. Combine the pasta with the cooked vegetables, broccoli and other seasonings then generously sprinkle with the parmesan cheese.

Pairs well with – Grilled chicken or fish or as a vegetarian dish on its own.

Cayman Islands

35. Seared Lionfish with Tropical Fruit Chutney

Once the spines, bones and veins have been carefully removed, the lionfish serves up extremely versatile options for fish dishes. This particular recipe is bursting with flavor from the various spices and seasonings incorporated into the fruit chutney.

Serves 6

Ingredients

6 lionfish fillets (6 oz each, seasoned with salt and pepper and seared until just cooked)
4 cup tropical fruit
1 cup apples (skin removed, diced into medium sized pieces, in acidulated water)
1 cup medium diced yellow onion
1 tsp minced garlic
1 tbsp sesame oil
2 tbsp vegetable oil
2 tbsp salt
1 tbsp curry powder
½ tsp ground ginger
¼ tsp allspice
½ tsp turmeric
¼ tsp Chinese five spice

2 tsps coriander
1 tbsp cardamom
¼ tsp cayenne pepper
½ tsp paprika
16 oz apple juice
12 oz pineapple juice
3 oz rice vinegar
2 oz mirin
3 oz honey
Whitewash (a flour and water mixture for thickening)

Preparation

1. On a medium flame, sauté the garlic and onions until they are cooked but not browned.
2. Adding all the spices, toast them then add all the liquids except the whitewash and boil.
3. Add the whitewash to thicken the mixture to a jelly-like consistency.
4. After cooling to room temperature, put in the apples and other fruit.
5. Slice each fillet into two lengthwise; place some of the chutney on one half then top with the other half.
6. Add some more chutney on top then serve.

Pairs well with – avocado and fresh greens or creamy potato salad

36. Cayman Triangle

These Cayman triangles are purely seafood based with a tenderized mahi mahi enveloped in crab and shrimp meat. They are the perfect appetizers which will have you looking forward with excitement to the remainder of any meal.

Serves 4 to 6

Ingredients

16 oz Mahi Mahi
8 oz crab meat
16 oz medium shrimp
4 tsps minced garlic
Salt and pepper

For sauce

2 cups heavy cream
1 cup Lemon juice
8 oz butter
Salt and pepper

Preparation

1. Beat the mahi mahi with a tenderizer and rub with the garlic, salt and pepper. Marinate.
2. Place the crab and shrimp along the length of the mahi mahi then roll to close. Hold in place with toothpicks.
3. Bake for twenty minutes at 350 °F or until finished.

For sauce

1. Reduce the cream over a low flame then add the butter and whisk.
2. Add the salt, pepper and lemon juice, then pour over mahi mahi to serve.

Pairs well with – lemon butter sauce, tartar sauce

Cuba

37. Medianoche

Medianoches are pork based sandwiches which are made with a soft and sweet bread called pan suave. Even in the absence of this bread other substitutes can be used such as challah rolls (6 inch), used in this recipe, these are similarly sweet and soft as pan suave.

Serves 4

Ingredients

¾ lb pork tenderloin (trim skin and extra fat)
Kosher salt
Black pepper
2 tbsp minced garlic cloves
2 oz olive oil
2 tbsp fresh orange juice
1 tbsp fresh lime juice
1 tsp dried oregano
½ tsp ground cumin
4 tbsp softened unsalted butter
1 tbsp yellow mustard
4 sweet rolls (cut in two lengthwise)
8 deli ham slices
32 dill pickle chips
8 Swiss cheese slices

Preparation

1. To prepare the pork, set the oven to 450 °F.
2. Poke holes in the pork and season it with salt and pepper then place the pork on a foil lined baking tray.
3. Put the garlic and the olive oil together in a small cup and microwave them for 45 seconds.
4. Pour the mixture into a bowl and in the orange juice and lime juice as well as the oregano, and cumin.
5. Pour the entire mixture all over the pork and rub some of it into the holes created by poking.
6. Place the pork into the oven on the middle rack and roast until an internal thermometer gives a reading of 145 F.
7. Remove a place on a cooling rack for half an hour. Then slice thinly and set aside.
8. To prepare the sandwiches mix half of the butter and all the mustard in a small dish.
9. Butter the rolls with the mixture.
10. Layer each bottom half of the rolls with pork, two ham slices, 8 pickles, two cheese slices then add the top half of the rolls.
11. Butter the top and bottom of the rolls with the leftover butter.
12. Using a frying pan on a medium flame, press the sandwiches down using a spatula until they are crispy and golden brown on both sides. (If you have a panini press this can be accomplished in a single step).

Pairs well with – fries, sweet potato fries, plantain chips

38. Ropa Vieja

This is Cuba's national dish and truly stands out with its bold flavor and beautiful colors. The English translation of this recipe's name is old clothes. It is called that because of the colorful appearance of the ingredients and the shredded meat which looks like old shredded rags.

Serves 6

Ingredients

1 tbsp vegetable oil
2 lbs beef flank
8 oz beef broth
8oz tomato sauce
1 small sliced onion
1 julienned green bell pepper
2 chopped garlic cloves
6 oz tomato paste
1 tsp ground cumin
1 tsp fresh cilantro (chopped)
1 tbsp olive oil
1 tbsp vinegar

Preparation

1. Heat the vegetable oil on a medium-high flame then brown the beef on both sides.
2. Place the beef into a slow cooker and add all the other ingredients.

3. Stir to blend well the cover and cook on high setting for 4 hrs. Alternatively cook on low for 10 hrs.
4. Shred meat to serve with the accompaniment of your choice.

Pairs well with – sour cream, rice, cilantro, cream cheese or tortillas

39. Pernil Asado Con Mojo

This well-seasoned pork will be allowed to marinate overnight to absorb the flavors of the seasonings for maximum impact.

Serves 10 -12

Ingredients

1 tablespoon oregano flakes
1 tablespoon ground cumin
30 chopped garlic cloves
16 oz freshly squeezed orange juice
16 oz fresh lime juice
7 to 9 lb pork shoulder (with bone in and skin still on)
Salt and ground black pepper

Preparation

1. Score the skin of the pork to make the pattern of a diamond.
2. Purée the oregano, garlic, cumin and 2 tablespoons of the orange juice in a food processor.
3. Rub this onto the pork along with salt and pepper and place in a bowl which can be covered.
4. Pour the orange and lime juices onto the pork. Cover and chill in the fridge overnight.
5. Take the pork out of the marinade and set the marinade aside for later use.

6. Season the pork with pepper and salt.
7. In an oven heated to 325 °F, place the pork with the skin upward in a roasting pan to which 16 ounces of water has been added.
8. Cover the pan with both parchment paper and foil. Allow the pork to bake until an internal thermometer reaches 180 °F (about 4 to 5 hrs).
9. Remove the wrappers then broil until the skin becomes crispy (about 5 to 10 mins).
10. Pour the juices from the marinade into a saucepan and reduce them until they thicken. Use as sauce to serve with the pork.

Pairs well with – white rice, fried ripe plantains, congri, green salad

40. Fricase de Pollo

This highly fragrant stew littered with potatoes and olives is beautifully spiced and has a flavor that is like no other. The chicken is so tender it falls right off the bones.

Serves 4 to 6

Ingredients

3 or 4 lb chicken pieces (preferably breasts and thighs with the skins removed)
1 teaspoon salt
½ teaspoon black pepper
½ teaspoon cumin
Garlic powder
1/3 cup olive oil
3 cup cubed red potatoes
1 large diced yellow onion
1 diced green bell pepper
6 minced garlic cloves
15 oz tomato sauce
2 packets Goya sazon seasoning
1 ½ cup white cooking wine
1 cup bitter orange juice
½ cup whole green olives
½ cup raisins
1 teaspoon oregano
2 bay leaves

Preparation

1. Sauté the onions, bell peppers and garlic until the onions become translucent.
2. Season the pieces of chicken with cumin and garlic powder.
3. Using a slow cooker, place the chicken along with all the ingredients and set on low for 6-8 hrs or on high for 4-5 hrs.
4. Alternatively, place all contents in a pressure cooker for 35 minutes on high.

Pairs well with - black beans and rice, brown rice, crusty bread

41. Cubano

This grilled ham and cheese sandwich is made with Cuban bread although French bread can also be used. The flavor infused roasted pork along with the cheese, pickles, ham and mustard is a Cuban tradition and was introduced in the early part of the 1900's. When Cubans emigrate to other parts of the world, they bring this tradition with them and so you will find this dish on the list of menu items at a Cuban restaurant.

Serves 4

Ingredients

1 loaf Cuban bread
Mustard or mayonnaise
1 lb sliced cooked ham
1 lb sliced roasted pork
½ lb sliced Swiss cheese
Sliced dill pickles (sliced)
Butter or cooking spray

Preparation

1. Place a frying pan or griddle to heat up on a medium flame.
2. Slice the bread into four equal pieces then further slice each piece diagonally.
3. Lather the slices with the mustard or mayo then layer with pork, cheese, ham, and pickles.
4. Make a light coating of spray or butter on the pan or griddle then place a sandwich on.

5. Use a heavy frying pan to flatten the sandwich as it grills. Try to flatten it to a third of its original thickness.
6. Leave the pan in place for a minute or two, then flip the sandwich and rest it again on top to grill the other side.
7. When the sandwich becomes golden brown it is finished. Slice diagonally to serve.

Pairs well with – green plantain chips, fries

42. Pescao en Escabeche

The key elements of escabeches are the vinegar and olive oil. The combination was used in Islamic Spain to pickle or flavor foods, meats and vegetables alike. In native Cuba, escabeches were commonly used to top fried sawfish. This recipe uses swordfish steaks along with bay leaves, onions, garlic and bell peppers.

Serves 6

Ingredients

6 8 oz swordfish steaks
12 cloves minced garlic
Salt and black pepper
2 cup flour
1 cup olive oil (extra virgin)
4 bay leaves
2 large sized green bell peppers cut up into ¼" rings
1 large sized yellow onion cut up into ¼" rings
16 oz white vinegar

Preparation

1. Use half of the garlic to season the fish along with the salt and pepper and let it rest for 20 minutes.
2. Dredge each piece of fish in the flour to properly coat them, shaking off the excess.

3. Place the oil to heat up on a medium high flame in a 12" frying pan.
4. Fry the fish steaks until they have browned on both sides.
5. After the fish has all been fried place them on a platter.
6. Add the remaining portion of garlic to the oil and stir until brown for about a minute.
7. Add the bay leaves, bell peppers and onions, stirring for about 4 minutes until cooked.
8. Add the vinegar and allow to boil, then cook for 2 more minutes.
9. Pour the mixture over the fish and rest for an hour before serving.

Pairs well with – white rice, fried green plantains, lettuce leaves, hard boiled eggs, olives

43. Elena Ruz

This sandwich is named after a young socialite from Cuba, Elena Ruz, who would give the waiter her instructions for making this particular sandwich. Since then the name has taken hold. The ideal bread to use is a white bread without crusts even though sweet rolls may be used as well.

Serves 1

Ingredients

2 white bread slices (toasted with crusts cut off)
4 oz cooked turkey, sliced
1 tbsp cream cheese
1 tbsp strawberry jam

Preparation

1. Spread the cream cheese generously on one slice of bread.
2. Spread strawberry jam on the other slice of bread.
3. Place the turkey between both slices of bread and enjoy.

Pairs well with - fried potato chips, fried green plantains

44. Torticas de Moron

The traditional way to make Torticas de Moron is with lard however in more recent times butter and shortening are being used. These Cuban sugar cookies can be had plain or with guava jelly in the middle.

Serves up 36 cookies

Ingredients

2 ½ cup all-purpose flour
1 tsp kosher salt
½ tsp baking powder
2 sticks unsalted butter
1 cup sugar
1 large egg
1½ tsps light rum
2 tsps finely grated zest of lime
5 tbsp guava jam

Preparation

1. Mix the flour, baking powder and salt together.

2. Using a mixer with the paddle attached, beat the butter for 1 minute then gradually add sugar until fluffy and light colored.

3. Add egg and beat for another minute then add lime zest and rum.

4. Add all of flour mixture to butter and stir with wooden spatula a few times.

5. Mix with hand mixer on low speed until all the flour is incorporated then stop.

6. Divide the cookie dough into two equal flat discs then wrap separately in plastic wrap and refrigerate for no less than 2 hours or until the next day.

7. Line a baking tray with grease paper and heat the oven to 350 °F.

8. Roll out one half of the dough between two sheets of wax paper to about ½" thickness then return to fridge to keep cold. Do the same with the second half.

9. Remove and cut out about 1 ½" rounds with a cookie cutter and place on tray. Use up all the extra scraps in the same way.

10. Make a small depression in the centre and keep cookies chilled until ready to fill.

11. Heat the jam on a low flame with constant stirring then strain if necessary.

12. Spoon a small amount of jam into the centre of each cookie (about ¼ tsp).

13. Bake for between 15 and 18 minutes. They will be a light golden brown. Serve when cooled.

Pairs well with - milk

Curacao

45. Kolo Stoba

This cabbage stew is a very popular dish in Curacao and boasts several types of meat. The use of annatto powder gives it the distinctive yellow orange color. The name Kolo Stoba is Papiamentu for cabbage stew.

Serves 6

Ingredients
1 large shredded cabbage
1 lb Salted Beef
1 lb pig's tail
1 lb goat meat
1 lb beef stew
3 potatoes, large
½ onion
1 tsp garlic powder
1 tsp nutmeg
1 cooking spoon butter
1 cooking spoon vinegar
1 tbsp ground annatto

Preparation

1. Soak the salted beef and pig's tail in water in a covered dish overnight in the fridge.

2. Thoroughly rinse all the meat and place in a pot filled with water along with the onion, nutmeg, annatto, garlic, vinegar and butter on a medium to high flame. (The next day)
3. Shred cabbage as the meat cooks, then pour hot water onto the cabbage after shredding.
4. Reduce the heat to low once the meats are cooked then add the cabbage.
5. Add a little sugar if desired and cook cabbage until softened.

Pairs well with - rice or funchi

46. Bolo di Glas

Bolo di glas or broken glass jello in English, is actually a combination of jello in various colors all set in a creamy white jello. The beautiful end result really does look like broken bits of glass and some versions include fruit in the creamy jello base. You have the freedom to play around with the color combinations as you like.

Serves 8

Ingredients

For colored gelatin

12 gelatin sheets
1 packet red gelatin
1 packet blue gelatin
1 packet yellow gelatin
Water

For creamy gelatin

10 gelatin sheets
16 oz coffee milk
1 can full cream sweetened condensed milk
½ tsp white vanilla
½ tsp almond essence
8 oz sour cream
Water

Preparation

Colored gelatin

1. Soak the gelatin sheets in some cold water for about 10 minutes until softened.

2. Add 8 ounces hot water to the red gelatin and dissolve 4 of the gelatin sheets into this mixture. Ensure that the gelatin sheets were properly squeezed.
3. Add 8 ounces cold water to the mix and stir well then pour into a mould and refrigerate until set.
4. Do the same with the other colored gelatin mixes.
5. When set un-mould and cut the gelatin up into cubes.

Creamy gelatin

1. Soak the gelatin sheets in cold water until soft.
2. Warm the milk on a low flame.
3. Squeeze the sheets properly and dissolve into the hot milk.
4. Add the condensed milk and sugar stirring well.
5. Add almond essence, vanilla and sour cream, beating well.
6. Cool the mixture.
7. Place gelatin cubes into a pudding shaped mould which has been oiled, then pour the white mixture over them.
8. Refrigerate overnight, then when set, carefully un-mould and serve on an appropriate dish.

Pairs well with – plain cake and ice cream

47. Banana Stoba

This ripe plantain stew offers an excellent blend of meat with vegetables enhanced by the spices; pimento, cloves and cinnamon. This sweet and spicy medley will be sure to please.

Serves 6

Ingredients

1 lb salted meat
3 ripe plantains
½ lb sweet potatoes
½ lb pumpkin
2 tbsp oil
2 tbsp butter
1 onion
2 stalks celery (cut into 1" pieces)
4 sticks cinnamon
10 whole pimentos
10 cloves
Sugar to taste

Preparation

1. Soak the meat overnight in the fridge.
2. Discard the water and place the meat in a sauce pan over medium heat to cook with water until tender.
3. Peel the plantains, potatoes and pumpkin and cut into 3" thick pieces. Set aside.
4. Sauté all the other ingredients except the sugar in a large pot then add all the contents of the meat pot.

5. After 10 minutes add the plantains, potatoes and pumpkin and cook on a medium flame until the vegetables are finished.
6. If the stew is too watery remove the vegetables and continue to cook until sauce has thickened then re-add vegetables. Add sugar as desired.

Pairs well with – cheese cornmeal croutons, rice

48. Bonchi Kora

This popular red kidney bean stew is traditionally cooked on Mondays on the island of Curacao. It is similarly popular in Aruba and Bonaire and always has a salted meat (usually beef) and pig's tail.

Serves 6

Ingredients

1 lb Red kidney beans
1 lb pig's tail
1 lb salted meat
1 large whole onion
3 chopped garlic cloves
2 stalks celery (cut up into 2"pieces)
¼ tsp nutmeg
1 tsp sugar
1 tsp butter

Preparation

1. Cut up the pig's tail and salted meat into 2" pieces and soak them overnight in the fridge.
2. The next day, throw off the water and place these in a large pot with fresh water. Cook on a medium flame until tender.
3. Remove the pig's tail leaving the salted meat to cook further.
4. Remove meat when tender and test the water for the amount of salt. Add a cup of salted water if required or add a cup of plain water if too salty. Do so until the right amount of saltiness is achieved.

5. Add the beans and all other contents and cook on a medium flame until the beans are tender. The end result should be a soupy consistency.

Pairs well with – white rice, bread, funchi

49. Pastechi

This flaky pastry can be filled with cheese, tuna, meat, vegetables or whatever your delight is. The key is not to make the filling moist so as not to ruin the flakiness of the dough. The versatility of this pastry makes it a perfect lunch, snack or appetizer item.

Serves 6 to 8

Ingredients

5 cup flour
5 tbsp butter
5 tbsp shortening
3 tbsp sugar
salt to taste
1 or 2 eggs (based on size)
8 to 12 oz cold water
Filling of choice

Preparation

1. Put all the ingredients together in to a bowl and knead into a smooth dough. Add a little flour if too sticky.
2. Cover the dough and rest for half an hour at room temperature.
3. Make small golf ball sized rounds out of the dough (or slightly bigger) then roll flat.
4. Add just the right amount of filling on one half then fold closed.

5. Seal the edges with a fork.
6. Fry them until golden brown and serve.

Pairs well with – bean dip, mustard, ketchup, green salad

50. Papaya Stoba

Another popular beef stew from Curacao which is one of their popular comfort foods. This entree is one the whole family can enjoy and even a few friends too.

Serves 4

Ingredients

1 lb stewing beef
1 tsp ground cumin
Soy sauce
Salt and pepper
1 green bell pepper, diced
2 diced medium onions
4 chopped tomatoes
1 lb papaya (green but almost orange, diced)
2 minced garlic gloves
Olive oil

Preparation

1. Marinate the beef in a mixture of cumin, salt, pepper, and soy sauce.
2. Brown the beef in a thick frying pan then set aside. Do it in two batches.
3. Add some more olive oil and sauté all the vegetables until the onions are cooked.
4. Reintroduce the beef and cover with water.

5   Allow to boil then reduce to a simmer (about an hour).

6   Add papaya and allow to simmer for about 15 minutes.

Pairs well with – rice, fresh cucumber salad, chopped chilli, pika

51. Balchi di Karni

Balchi di Karni is the term used in Curacao for meat balls. This particular method of preparation gives it an interesting flavor with the sweetness of the mango chutney incorporated into the balls themselves as well as the sauce.

Serves 4 to 6

Ingredients

For meatballs

1 ½ lb ground beef
2 tbsp butter
1 onion, chopped
⅓ bell pepper, chopped
½ tsp garlic powder
Pinch salt
½ tsp cumin
½ tsp Goya complete seasoning
1 tbsp all-purpose seasoning
1 tsp mango chutney
1 tsp Italian seasoning
3 white bread slices
2 eggs, beaten

For sauce

1 onion, chopped
1 tomato, chopped
⅔ bell pepper, chopped
1 meat cube
½ tsp cumin
½ tsp Goya complete seasoning

½ tsp curry powder
1 tbsp pickles
1 tsp mango chutney
2 tsps tomato paste
1 tbsp soy sauce
4 oz water

Preparation

Meatballs

1. Fry the onions and pepper in the butter until they are soft.
2. Soak the bread in water for a few minutes.
3. Remove the crusts, squeeze the water out and break them up into pieces.
4. Combine the onions, garlic powder, pepper, cumin, salt, Goya seasoning, mango chutney, all-purpose seasoning and Italian seasoning together and mix into the ground beef.
5. Add in the bread and eggs and all the other seasonings.
6. Shape the beef into balls and press slightly flat.
7. Heat some oil in a skillet and fry the meat balls, both sides until browned and tender.
8. Take 6 tablespoons of the oil from frying the meatballs to use for the sauce.

Sauce

1. Heat the oil to fry the onions, tomatoes and peppers until they are soft.
2. Add the meat cube, cumin, Goya seasoning and curry, mix and allow to simmer for half a minute.
3. Add all the other sauce ingredients and mix them in well. Cook for another couple of minutes.
4. Put the meatballs in and let the sauce simmer for 1 more minute on a medium flame.

Pairs well with – rice, spaghetti, rice and beans

52. Tutu

This traditional recipe serves as a side dish or an appetizer at meal time. The original recipe comes from Africa and much like funchi is cornmeal based. The addition of black eyed peas adds protein to the mix.

Serves 8 to 10

Ingredients

1 lb Black eye peas
6 cup water
2 chopped garlic cloves (or 1 tsp garlic powder)
1 tsp salt
¾ cup sugar
8 oz Coconut milk
1¾ cup corn meal
2 tbsp butter

Preparation

1. Wash the peas and soak them for 2 hrs.
2. Drain and add the peas, 6 cups of water and chopped garlic to a sauce pan. Boil slowly on a medium flame.
3. When beans are tender, add more water if necessary, add salt, coconut milk and sugar and cook for 10 minutes more.
4. Gradually add the cornmeal with constant stirring to mix the peas in properly with the cornmeal. The cornmeal should be cooked after twenty minutes.

5. Add butter then stir it in well then turn off heat. Spoon the tutu into a damp dish and cover with another damp dish and flatten between them.

Pairs well with – cheese, saltfish

53. Repa di Pampuna

This popular and well-loved snack is actually a pumpkin pancake. It can be had savoury or sweet. They are also much smaller than regular pancakes.

Serves 4

Ingredients

1 lb pumpkin
3 oz full cream milk
2 eggs
¾ cup self-raising flour
2 tbsp melted butter
2 tbsp vanilla sugar
2 tbsp granulated sugar
2 tsps baking powder
½ tsp salt
½ tsp cinnamon
Nutmeg

Preparation

1. Peel the pumpkin and cut into large pieces for boiling.
2. Boil in salt water for 20 minutes. Pour off water and allow to cool.
3. Add milk, eggs, butter and vanilla sugar. Stir well.
4. Add the flour, baking powder, cinnamon, salt and nutmeg. Mix and rest batter for 20 mins. (Batter will be thicker than for regular pancakes)

5. Pour some oil in a skillet and fry a half tablespoon of the batter at a time until both sides are golden brown.

Pairs well with – maple syrup

Dominica and Dominican Republic

54. Sancocho

Sancocho is a culinary treasure of the Dominican people. It is customarily had on special occasions and takes quite a bit of time to prepare, due to all the ingredients it contains. The traditional way to prepare it is with beef however there is a seven meat version as well. This recipe is the deluxe seven meat version however you can opt for using a single meat only.

Serves 8

Ingredients

1 lb beef for stewing
1 lb goat meat
1 lb pork sausage
1 lb pork for stewing
1 lb chicken
1 lb pork ribs
1 lb smoked ham bones
Juice from 2 limes
1 teaspoon chopped cilantro or parsley
1/2 teaspoon powdered oregano
1 teaspoon mashed garlic
1 ½ teaspoon salt
4 tbsp oil
2 ½ quarts water
½ lb yam name (cut up into 1" pieces)
½ lb pumpkin (cut up into 1" pieces)

½ lb taro yautia (cut up into 1" pieces)
3 green plantains (cut 2 of them into 1" pieces)
½ lb cassava (cut up into 1" pieces)
2 cobs corn (cut them into ½"slices)

Preparation

1. Cut all of the meats into little pieces and coat them with lime juice (excluding the sausage). Keep them separate.
2. Put the beef into a large dish and add cilantro, garlic, oregano and ½ tsp salt. Season well and marinate for at least half hour.
3. Heat some oil in a large sauce pan on a medium flame and add the beef. Stir and cover to simmer for about ten minutes. If the beef seems as if it will burn add a little water.
4. Now add in the pork and simmer further for fifteen minutes. Add water where necessary.
5. Excluding the chicken, add the other meats and simmer for 15 minutes more. Add more water when necessary.
6. Now add the chicken and continue cooking for five minutes. Add water where necessary.
7. Pour 2 quarts water into the sauce pan and allow to boil.
8. Add in the yam, pumpkin, yautía and two cut up plantains and simmer with the cover on for fifteen minutes.

9. Grate the last plantain and add to saucepan as well as all the other ingredients not yet added with the exception of the salt. Add water as needed and stir often to prevent too much sticking.
10. Simmer until all the ingredients you added are cooked through. Add salt as desired.

Pairs well with – White rice, avocado

55. Mangu

This is a favorite of Dominicans and is usually eaten as a breakfast item. In English it is known as mashed plantains.

Serves 4

Ingredients

3 green plantains
1 Qt. water
2 oz olive oil
1 cup white onion, sliced
1 ½ tbsp salt
1 cup sliced peppers (Anaheim)

Preparation

1. Boil the plantains in the skin for twenty minutes until tender yet firm.
2. Drain the liquid and save a cup for later.
3. Cool and peel the plantains.
4. Sauté the onions in a heated frying pan in oil until they are tender. Use medium heat.
5. Mash the plantains in a bowl using some of the kept liquid and a little salt.

6. Place in food processor or blender and add the peppers then puree.
7. Top the mashed plantains with the onions to serve.

Pairs well with – eggs, salami, fried cheese

56. Arroz Blanco

White rice is a normal part of the traditional Dominican lunch. Dominicans pride themselves on being able to cook the perfect white rice. It may sound simple but even the simplest element of a meal when well-prepared makes a world of difference.

Serves 4

Ingredients

5 tbsp vegetable oil
1 ¼ tsp salt
6 cup water
4 cup long grain rice

Preparation

1. Heat half of the oil and all the salt on a medium flame in a cast iron pot. (Aluminium may be used as well).
2. Add all the water carefully being mindful of splatters.
3. Rinse rice under running water and drain.
4. When the water starts to boil add the rice stirring at regular intervals.
5. When the dries water begins to dry off, cover the pot with a well-fitting lid. Simmer on low flame.

6. Add the remaining oil after 15 minutes, then stir and cover once more.
7. Rice should be ready after five minutes, however and additional five minutes on low heat may be given for it to reach perfection.

Pairs well with – seafood, meat, beans

57. Habichuelas Guisadas

Another popular part of Dominican cuisine are the Habichuelas or Dominican beans. They even form a part of "the Dominican flag" or la Bandera Dominicana which is typically a lunch meal of rice, meat and beans. The flavors can be varied based on preference.

Serves 4

Ingredients

2 cup dry beans (pinto, red kidney or cranberry beans may be used)
1 tbsp olive oil
Oregano
1 chopped bell pepper
1 red onion, small (sliced into four)
2 crushed garlic cloves
1 cup diced West Indies pumpkin
1 cup tomato sauce
Chopped celery stalk leaves
4 sprigs thyme
½ tsp fresh cilantro, chopped
salt to taste)

Preparation

1. Pre-soak the beans overnight.
2. Boil in fresh water until soft. May use pressure cooker.
3. Remove the beans from the water and reserve both.

4. Heat oil on a medium flame and add all the ingredients except the beans and salt.
5. Cook for 30 seconds while stirring then add the beans and let them simmer for 2 minutes.
6. Add the bean water (should be 6 cups. If not, top up with regular water).
7. Mash the beans and cook until creamy. Add salt to taste.

Pairs well with – white rice, salad, meat

58. Pollo Guisado

Chicken is very popular meat for people of the Dominican Republic as well as across the wider Caribbean region It cooks fairly quickly, is economical, versatile to prepare and widely available. Braising it is a favorite method of preparation among Dominicans. This pollo guisado has an Italian flair.

Serves 6

Ingredients

2 lb chicken (cut up into little pieces)
2 limes, halved
Oregano
1 sml. red onion, julienned
½ cup chopped celery (if desired)
Salt
½ tsp mashed garlic
2 tbsp oil
1 tsp granulated sugar
16 oz water
4 plum tomatoes, quartered
2 green bell peppers (or cubanelles)
¼ cup seedless olives, halved (if desired)
1 cup tomato sauce
Small bunch cilantro leaves
¼ tsp pepper

Preparation

1. Thoroughly rub the chicken with the limes.

2. Season with oregano, celery, onion, salt and garlic then allow to marinate for half an hour.
3. Heat the oil in a saucepan on a medium flame and add the sugar.
4. Add chicken when the sugar browns but leave all the seasonings in the marinade. Sauté until slightly brown.
5. Add 6 teaspoons of water, cover and simmer on medium for fifteen minutes. Stir in between and add water as necessary.
6. Add all the vegetables from the marinade, cover and simmer until they are cooked. Add water as necessary.
7. Add in the tomato sauce and a quarter of the water then simmer on.
8. Add the cilantro, salt and pepper and serve.

Pairs well with – white rice, salad, beans

59. Ensalada Verde

Green Salad or Ensalada verde is a regular part of Dominican lunch. It increases the nutritive value of the usual rice, beans and meat meals and is very easy to prepare.

Serves 6

Ingredients

2 sliced or diced tomatoes

½ lettuce or ¼ shredded cabbage

1 diced or sliced cucumber

1 julienned bell pepper

1 small julienned onion (if desired)

1 boiled and sliced beetroot (if desired)

For Dressing

9 teaspoons fruit vinegar

9 teaspoons olive oil

Salt to taste

Preparation

1. Place the vegetables nicely on a serving dish.
2. Combine vinegar, oil and salt in a container and shake.
3. Serve salad with dressing on the side.

Pairs well with – Rice, beans, chicken or other meat

60. Tostones

The Dominican tostones, green fries or fritos verdes are a well-loved side. They are made from green plantains which have been fried twice and flattened in between frying. They are well paired with various dips and are popular in households and with street vendors. This recipe has an accompanying dip to complete the experience.

Serves 4

Ingredients

2 green plantains
4 oz oil
Salt to taste
For Dip
1 chopped tomato
4 parsley sprigs
1 clove of garlic
¼ teaspoon pepper
3tsps olive oil

Preparation

For tostones

1. Peel plantains and cut 1" thick rounds.
2. Heat the oil in a frying pan and fry on both sides until golden.

3. Flatten or press the plantains with a fork or bottle to about a quarter inch.
4. Return to the oil and fry until golden once more. Serve hot.

For Dip

1. Blend the dip ingredients together thoroughly but stop before it completely liquefies.

Pairs well with – guasacaca sauce, avocado ranch dip, fried fish, guacamole

61. Habichuelas con Dulce

This bean based dessert is made up of some very interesting components. Combining beans with milk is not exactly an idea that would readily pop into the mind. For many, the taste may have to be acquired but for Dominicans it is familiar and a favorite. Such is the creative license of food. Explore your adventurous side with this sweet treat!

Serves 8

Ingredients

4 cup red kidney beans boiled soft (may use pinto or cranberry beans)
6 cup water from the boiled beans
16 oz coconut milk
24 oz evaporated milk
½ teaspoon salt
1 cup sugar
1 teaspoon vanilla
2 sticks cinnamon
10 whole cloves
½ lb sweet potatoes, cubed
½ cup raisins

Preparation

1. Blend the beans with their water until smooth then strain to remove any solids.

2. Pour the puree and all the other ingredients, excluding the raisins into a sauce pan and simmer on a low flame until potatoes are cooked. Frequently stir.
3. Add raisins and continue to simmer for a further 10 minutes.
4. Take cinnamon sticks and cloves out and remove from heat.
5. Cool the liquid to room temperature and chill to serve.

Pairs well with – milk, cookies, cassava bread

Grenada

62. Callaloo Soup

Callaloo was first brought to the Caribbean from Africa through the slave trade. There are many versions of this soup across the Caribbean making use of other greens. On some islands it is also known as pepper pot soup with the addition of a meat or meats. This delicious Grenadian version is ideal for vegetarians with the addition of coconut milk and serves as an excellent starter for any meal.

Serves 8

Ingredients

4 tablespoons butter
1 large finely chopped onion
2 large crushed garlic cloves
450 g washed and chopped callaloo

5 to 6 finely chopped okra
¼ cup coconut cream
3 to 4 fresh thyme sprigs
1 teaspoon sugar
8 oz water
Salt and pepper

Preparation

1. Placing the butter in a big pot sauté the onions until softened, then add garlic and sauté until softened but not brown.
2. Add in the chopped callaloo, okras, cream, thyme and sugar and place a well-fitting lid on. Cook for half an hour.
3. Take thyme out and blend the contents in a blender.
4. Pour soup back into pot and add the water. Cook for 10 minutes more, then serve.

Pairs well with – toasted bread

63. Lambie Souse

The conch is a very popular seafood item served across the Caribbean. The snail inside is called lambie in Grenada. Because of the thickness of the meat, it generally has to be tenderized before cooking as it can be extremely tough or hard to chew if this is not done. The empty shell has been used to make a very effective horn and is popularly used during cricket matches as a noisemaker. In this recipe, the souse is a liquid made up for pickling, into which the cooked lambies will be soaked.

Serves 8 to 12

Ingredients

3 to 4 lambies
4 oz lime juice
2 large sliced up onions
2 crushed cloves garlic
2 small sliced up cucumbers
½ cut up hot pepper
2 whole limes
Salt to taste

Preparation

1. Wash the lambies very well with the two limes then soften using a metal tenderizer.

2. Boil with garlic for an hour and a half to two hours then cool.

3. Slice the lambies thinly.

4. Make up a mixture of 32 ounces of water, salt, lime juice, onions, cucumbers and peppers, then add the sliced lambies.

5. Leave to steep covered for an hour and a half to two hours.

Pairs well with - crackers

64. Peleau

Peleau is a convenient one pot meal enjoyed across the Caribbean in islands like Trinidad, Antigua, St, Vincent and Guyana. In Guyana, it is called 'Cook up' and in the southern Unites States their version of it is 'Jambalaya'. A delicious complete meal, peleau consists of chicken or meat and sausage in some cases, peas and definitely coconut milk. The caramelized sugar is another signature component which imparts color and flavor.

Serves 4 to 6

Ingredients

3 tbsp vegetable oil
3/4 cup sugar
2 ½ to 3 lbs cut up chicken (may also use goat's meat or beef)
1 chopped onion
1 clove minced garlic
1½ cup soaked pigeon peas (or black-eyed peas)
2 cup rice
24 oz water
8 oz coconut milk
2 cup cubed Hubbard squash
2 chopped carrots
¼ cup chopped parsley
1 tsp dried thyme
1 bunch chopped scallions
2 oz ketchup
3 tbsp butter

Preparation

1. In a frying pan on a high flame, heat the oil and add the sugar allowing it to caramelize. Stir constantly.
2. Add in the chicken then stir to coat all the pieces properly with the burnt sugar.
3. Turn the flame down to medium and add in the garlic and onions, cooking for a minute.
4. Drain the water from the peas, pour them into the pan then add the rice, coconut milk and water. Reduce the flame further and simmer covered for half an hour.
5. Add in the other vegetables and seasonings, stirring well and cooking for an additional 20 minutes to half an hour.

Pairs well with – avocado, tossed salad, sliced tomatoes

65. Cocoa Tea

The Grenadian version of hot chocolate is known as cocoa tea. The same is true across the Caribbean. It is made from the chocolate balls or sticks formed from the cocoa plant, and is nicely spiced to give the true flavors of the Caribbean. A common feature are the oils which float on top after the tea has been boiled. Be careful if having piping hot as the oils increase the temperature phenomenally.

Serves 2 to 3

Ingredients

2 cocoa balls
16 oz water
4 to 8 oz milk
sugar
Spices
Cinnamon stick
bay leaf
ground nutmeg
cloves

Preparation

1. Bring the water to a rolling boil and grate the balls into it. You can also just drop the balls into the water as they will dissolve.
2. Add the spices and continue to simmer for about 10 minutes.

3. Strain and pour into cup or mug.
4. Sweeten with milk and sugar as desired.

Pairs well with – breakfast, sweet potato pone

66. Sweet Potato Pone

This is a popular recipe all across the Caribbean and has Amerindian roots. Made mainly from sweet potatoes and grated coconut, some other islands add other starch ingredients such as yam or cassava. It is generally enjoyed as a dessert or snack, is well spiced and may or may not contain raisins.

Serves 8

Ingredients

20 oz milk
2 ½ cup sugar
½ tsp salt
3 tsps ginger
½ tsp nutmeg
½ cup grated tannia (alternatively use new cocoyam, yautía or dasheen)
1 ½ tsps cinnamon
4 cup grated sweet potatoes
1 ½ cup grated coconut

Preparation

1. Mix all the ingredients thoroughly together and pour into a greased baking tin.
2. Glaze the top with sugar and water.

3. Bake for at least an hour and a half at 350 degrees °F.

Pairs well with – rum sauce, whipped cream

67. Nutmeg Ice Cream

This nutmeg ice cream is reminiscent of eggnog and makes use of one of the spice island's popular spices, the nutmeg. Once grated, the nutmeg releases oils which impart a strong flavor that is much more potent than the powdered ground bottled nutmeg. You will certainly appreciate its outstanding taste in this homemade ice cream.

Serves 4

Ingredients

20 oz milk
20 oz heavy cream
3 eggs, large
3/4 cup sugar
1 tsp just grated nutmeg
1/8 tsp salt
1/4 tsp vanilla

Preparation

1. Boil the milk and cream together then whisk in the nutmeg, sugar, vanilla and salt.
2. Remove 4 ounces of the milk mixture and mix into the beaten eggs, then add this back to the pot.
3. Cook on a medium flame with constant stirring using a wooden spoon.

4. When a thermometer reads 175 °F remove from flame and pour the mixture into a metal dish that has been placed into a larger container with ice and cold water.
5. Stir the mixture until it becomes cold then freeze it in an ice cream freezer based on instructions.

Pairs well with – shredded coconut, cookies

Guadeloupe

68. Black Bean Chicken

Guadeloupe's cuisine is a fusion of African, French, East Indian and South east Asian cultures. This easy to make chicken features lemon juice, cumin, jalapeno pepper and garlic and takes under an hour to prepare.

Serves 6

Ingredients

3 ½ lbs cut up chicken
Ground black pepper
3 tsps Olive oil
½ cup chopped onion
½ cup chopped green pepper
1 chopped Jalapeno (no seeds)
1 large minced clove garlic
1 tsp ground cumin
1 medium peeled and chopped tomato
3 tsps lemon juice
15 oz black beans

Preparation

1. Season chicken with black pepper and sauté in olive oil for 3 minutes on either side. Remove and set aside.

2. To the pan add the onions, bell pepper, jalapeno and garlic.
3. Cook them for 2 minutes then add the cumin, chopped tomatoes, lemon juice and beans.
4. Reintroduce chicken to pot and simmer for twenty minutes covered.
5. Take lid off and cook uncovered for another ten minutes.

Pairs well with - rice

69. Caribbean Ginger Turkey

This flavorful broiled or barbecued turkey breast delivers excellent flavor with a sweet and slightly gingery punch. Interestingly this recipe has no salt apart from that which the soy sauce provides and so it is a healthy meal option.

Serves 4

Ingredients

2 lb turkey de-skinned breast
2 oz soy sauce
2 oz dry sherry
2 tbsp apricot jam
½ teaspoon ginger
4 oz water
¼ cup brown sugar
2 tbsp vegetable oil
2 tsps lemon juice
1 clove chopped garlic

Preparation

1. Remove the turkey breast bone and cartilage carefully.
2. Cut the breast into 3 portions and shake in a ziploc bag with all the ingredients.

3. Rest the bag in a container and marinate overnight in the fridge or at least four hours.
4. Take the breasts out and reserve the marinade.
5. Cook the turkey by broiling or barbecuing for twelve to fifteen minutes. Occasionally turn and brush with the marinade.

Pairs well with – white rice, fried ripe plantains, rice and peas, steamed vegetables, sliced fruit

70. Pineapple Chicken Rundown

The key ingredient in rundown is coconut milk. It gives the dish a creamy appearance with an excellent flavor. This chicken dish is truly tropical with the use of pineapples and may even remind you of a pina colada!

Serves: 2

Ingredients

2 boneless chicken (season with thyme, salt and pepper)
3 oz fresh pineapple chunks, diced
6 oz coconut rundown sauce
2 tbsp double cream
1 fresh hollowed out pineapple cut into two lengthwise

Preparation

1. Grill the chicken breasts on both sides for eight to ten minutes.
2. Combine the rundown sauce with the pineapple chunks and double cream and heat them together.
3. Spoon the rundown into the pineapple halves and serve.

Pairs well with - mashed potatoes, diced papaya

71. Stuffed Cabbage Leaves

These cabbage rolls are not difficult to make. The preparation just takes a little bit of time. Instead of boiling the whole cabbage, it can be frozen overnight then thawed the next day to soften the leaves. It is usually served at special occasions and best with leaner ground beef.

Serves 6

Ingredients

2 lb light cabbage
4 large garlic cloves
1 cup rice
2 tsps fresh mint
1 lb minced beef
2 oz lemon juice
Salt and pepper
2 oz butter

Preparation

1. Remove centre stem of cabbage and boil until the leaves can roll easily.
2. Separate the leaves in a colander.
3. Cut each leaf lengthwise along the ribs.
4. Mix the rice, butter, ground beef and seasonings together.

5. Place a tablespoon of the mixture along a rib and spread it to the entire length of the leaf and roll as you would a Swiss roll.
6. Gently squeeze each roll when placing in pan.
7. Arrange the rolls compactly in a pot and sprinkle them with the garlic and salt between each roll.
8. Pour water into the pot up to the level of the cabbage and cook for fifteen to twenty minutes with the lid on. Use medium flame.
9. Crush a garlic clove with some mint and salt, add lemon juice and pour onto the cabbage.
10. Simmer until the rice has cooked.

Pairs well with – rice, tangy tomato sauce

Haiti

72. Poule en Sauce

This Haitian stew can be cooked in various ways and is generally served with rice. This particular method uses a Creole sauce as the stew base and has a spicy and tangy flavor.

Serves 4 to 6

Ingredients

1 lb Chicken
½ diced onion
2 tsps minced Garlic
3 tsps lime juice
4 fresh thyme sprigs
4 fresh parsley sprigs
1 whole scotch bonnet pepper
1 teaspoon black pepper
½ red bell pepper, juliennned
1 chicken bouillon cube
1 tablespoon seasoning salt
4 oz white vinegar
2 tablespoons tomato paste

Preparation

1. Clean the chicken with lemon and vinegar and then rinse it with hot water.

2. Mix the garlic, thyme, parsley, black pepper, bouillon cube, and seasoning salt and rub the chicken with it. Rest for fifteen minutes or marinate overnight in the fridge.

3. Brown the chicken on both sides in a large pot and add 4 ounces of water as well as the onions, tomato paste and all the peppers.

4. Cook the chicken on a high flame for twenty-five minutes then reduce to low and simmer until serving time.

Pairs well with – white rice

73. Bannann Bouyi

This side dish is so simple and is a common part of Haitian meals. It is popular across the Caribbean also, originally coming from West Africa. It is available all year long.

Serves 1

Ingredients

24 oz water
1 green plantain
1 teaspoon salt

Preparation

1. Put the water to boil in a pot with salt.
2. Wash the plantains with cold water and cut the small ends off either side.
3. Cut 1 inch off each end of the plantain.
4. Score the plantain from top to bottom then cut in half and boil for 20 minutes.
5. When completely boiled remove the skin and serve with main meal.

Pairs well with – scrambled eggs, stewed chicken

74. Espageti

Espageti or Haitian spaghetti is generally made with sausages or smoked herring. This is a nice after school meal and can also be served for breakfast as well as lunch. This recipe also allows for customization so you can add other ingredients to make it your own.

Serves 4

Ingredients

1 lb spaghetti
½ lb pork sausage, spicy
1 small sliced onion
½ diced green bell pepper
2 tbsp tomato paste
½ minced scotch bonnet pepper
1 teaspoon all-purpose seasoning
2 thyme sprigs
1 chicken bouillon cube
2 tbsp olive oil
32 oz water
3 tsps salt

Preparation

1. Boil the water with a tablespoon of olive oil and two teaspoons salt added in a large saucepan.
2. Cook the spaghetti until just right (al dente) then drain and reserve for later.

3. Sauté the sausages in the same saucepan in the remaining olive oil for about three minutes.
4. Add the remaining seasoning and sauté for another three minutes.
5. Add 8 ounces of water, bring to boil and then add the spaghetti mixing in well.
6. Turn the heat down simmer for a few minutes then serve.

Pairs well with – bread and butter

75. Sos Pwa

Sos pwa is Haiti's version of black bean soup which can also be varied by using other types of beans. This savoury dish can easily become a favorite. It is mainly a puree with a few whole beans.

Serves 8

Ingredients

16 oz black beans
8 oz coconut milk
1 tbsp salt
1 tbsp pepper
2 tbsp olive oil
1 teaspoon ground cloves
1 chicken bouillon cube
8 cups water

Preparation

1. Boil the water and beans in a large pot until soft. Top up with more water as the need arises.
2. Take ¾ of the beans out and place in a blender with some of the boiling water and puree.
3. Run the pureed beans through a sieve then pour back into the pot.

4. Add the other ingredients and slowly stir.
5. Cook for 15 minutes on a low flame then serve when ready.

Pairs well with – white rice

Jamaica

76. Jerk Chicken

A succulent chicken dish with a unique smoky flavor, Jerk chicken dishes are a staple of Jamaica and are well-known throughout the world.
Serves 4

Ingredients

One whole 3lb chicken or 3lb of chicken breasts
6 sliced scotch bonnet peppers
3 Medium onions (finely chopped)
8 Cloves garlic, (finely chopped)
2 Tablespoon of thyme
2 Tablespoon ground allspice
2 Tablespoon sugar
2 Tablespoon salt
2 Tablespoon black pepper
2 Tablespoon of cinnamon
2 Tablespoon of nutmeg
2 Tablespoon of ginger
1 cup orange juice
1/2 cup olive oil
1 cup white vinegar
1/2 cup soy sauce
1 lime (for juice)

Preparation

1. Chop the garlic, peppers and onions.
2. Next add all the ingredients, except the chicken into a blender, this makes the jerk sauce.

3. Now cut the chicken into 4 pieces.
4. Rub the sauce into the chicken, however leave some excess for dipping and basting later. The chicken now needs to be left to marinade overnight.
5. On the next day the chicken is ready to cook in the oven for 1 hour, 30 minutes each side.
6. While the chicken is cooking, baste with some of the remaining marinade.
7. Each quarter chicken needs to be cut into 5 or so smaller pieces. You will need something very sharp in order to cut the flesh and bone.

Pairs well with – rice and peas, dumplings or festival.

77. Curry Goat

Curry goat is a tender goat meat curry with fantastic flavors and aromas. An absolute favorite with Jamaican's and West Indian's alike. The food of choice at any celebration.

Serves 4

Ingredients

1kg goat meat (remove bones)
3 tomatoes
1 Scotch bonnet
1 tablespoon salt
1/2 teaspoon dried thyme
1/2 teaspoon Allspice
1 teaspoon freshly ground black pepper
3 tablespoon curry powder
2 whole spring onions, sliced
1 onion, sliced
3 cloves of garlic, crushed
4 tablespoons oil
juice of 1 lime
1 tin of coconut milk

Preparation

1. Use half a lime to cover the goat meat.
2. Place the meat in a substantial bowl, add the salt, pepper, thyme, allspice, curry powder, garlic spring onion, onion and Scotch bonnet. Marinate for 2 hours in the fridge.

3. Heat the oil in a frying pan with a medium-heat until very hot, add the meat to the pan only
4. Cook the meat until brown for around 5-6 minutes, then add all the seasoning mix and cook for a further 2 minutes.
5. Next add the tomatoes and cook until everything is combined for about 3 more minutes.
6. Add the coconut milk and around 2 more cups of water.
7. Reduce the heat to low and bring to the boil, then cover and cook until meat is tender. This will probably take a couple of hours.
8. Finally, Stir in the remaining lime juice.

Pairs well with – rice and peas or plain white rice.

78. Ackee and Saltfish

Ackee and Saltfish is the national dish of Jamaica and hugely popular. Since Ackee is a fruit, this dish can be eaten for breakfast, lunch or dinner.

Serves 4

Ingredients

1 Tin of Ackee
1 teaspoon chicken stock powder
1 Onion roughly chopped
2 Fresh tomatoes
1 teaspoon Black Pepper
1 Knob of butter (optional)
1 Packet of salted cod fish.
1 Scotch bonnet (optional - for extra heat)

Preparation

1. Use a saucepan, add water and the salted cod and boil.
2. Pour off the water and repeat 1-2 more times, depending on taste.
3. Next pour some more cold water onto fish and leave for 5, then drain.
4. Flake the fish into s9mall pieces
5. Take a frying pan, add the oil, tomatoes, onion and scotch bonnet (optional) and fry until soft.

6. Add the fish flakes along with the chicken stock mix in water adding the butter.
7. Cook for around 3-4 minutes.
8. Add the Ackee, and sprinkle with black pepper to season. Be sure to simmer on low heat for 3-5 minutes.
Your Ackee and saltfish is ready to serve.

Pairs well with – plantains (boiled or fried).

79. Sorrel

Sorrel drink is a Jamaican beverage that was typically had only at Christmas time because sorrel is an annual plant. It is now dried and stored so as this aromatic drink can be enjoyed all year round. There is a white and red variety of this plant, of which the red is more potent with flavor.

Serves 8

Ingredients

1 ½ C dried sorrel
2 inches finely chopped and peeled ginger root
3 cloves
5 ¾ C water
¾ C sugar
1 ½ C amber rum
2 C ice cubes

Preparation

1. Pour 5 cups of boiling water over the sorrel, cloves and ginger in a heat resistant container. Steep for four hours or the next day.
2. Boil the sugar with the remaining water to dissolution and cool.
3. Strain the steeped liquid into a drink jug and stir in the dissolved sugar, rum and ice.

Pairs well with – dark fruit cake, any meal

80. Irish Moss

The seaweed, Irish Moss, was discovered in Ireland and the drink was widely consumed during the 19th century famine in Ireland. The weed came to Jamaica with the Irish who had emigrated there and now the weed grows by the sea on rocks. The drink is believed to confer sexual stamina to its drinkers and so is popular among men in Jamaica. It has also been used for medicinal purposes.

Serves 8

Ingredients

¾ lb Irish moss
3 oz gum arabic
¾ cup honey or 1 tin sweetened condensed milk
¾ lbs sugar
5 oz isinglass
5 oz linseed
3 tbsp vanilla
5 quarts water
2 tbsp grated nutmeg

Preparation

1. Wash well the Irish moss and soak in water until the next day. Use two parts of water for every part of Irish moss.
2. Put the 5 quarts of water to boil and add the soaked moss, linseed, gum Arabic and isinglass.

3. Boil for 45 minutes then pour the liquid through a strainer into a jug.
4. The other contents should have dissolved leaving the moss which is to be discarded.
5. Add the sweeteners, vanilla and nutmeg then stir. Boil again for ten minutes.
6. Cool the mixture then refrigerate for at least five hours prior to serving.

Pairs well with – steamed fish

81. Carrot Juice

This drink was once a must in Jamaican households with Sunday dinner. When sweetened with condensed milk, a dark alcoholic stout may be added like Guinness or dragon. There is another version where lime juice and sugar are used to sweeten instead of condensed milk.

Serves 4

Ingredients

2 lb carrots
5 cup water
8 oz condensed milk
1 tsp grated nutmeg
1 tsp vanilla

Preparation

1. Scrape the carrot skins and cut them into pieces then blend.
2. Strain and throw the pulp away.
3. Sweeten with condensed milk and spice with vanilla and nutmeg. Stir well.
4. Serve over crushed ice.

Pairs well with – rice and peas and chicken

Martinique

82. Accra

Accra are fritters which can be made with salt fish, vegetables and even prawns. Each island puts their own spin on it with some even adding curry powder. These fritters commonly serve as breakfast, a meal starter or a snack.

Serves 4

Ingredients

8 oz flaked and de-salted cod fish
2 tbsp oil
1 minced onion
1 grated garlic clove
Hot pepper powder
Finely chopped green onions
8 oz flour
2 tsps baking powder
Room temperature water
Oil for frying

Preparation
1. Sauté the onions in a heated frying pan for three minutes, then add the garlic, peppers and green onions, cooking for another two minutes.

2. Mix with the flaked cod fish in a bowl.
3. In a separate bowl mix the flour and baking powder together then add the seasoned cod plus water to form a thickened batter.
4. Deep fry in a pan with very hot oil. Turn flame on medium setting.
4. Use a tablespoon to drop the batter and cook both sides until browned. Use paper towels for draining.

Pairs well with – chutney, pepper sauce or Ti-punch

83. Boudin

Boudin is a sausage which is traditionally eaten in Martinique at Christmas time. There are two types, the creole version and the blanc version. This recipe is the blanc version which uses pork and liver. Other meats may also be added such as prawns, conch, crabs or fish.

Serves 8

Ingredients

1 ½ lb pork steak
½ lb fresh pig's liver
1 coarsely chopped onion
3 whole garlic cloves
2 bay leaves
1 fresh thyme sprig
Water
Salt to taste
Black pepper to taste
2 cup long grain rice
1 bunch thinly sliced green onions
½ cup finely chopped Italian parsley
Cayenne pepper

Preparation

1. Slice the pork and liver into 2 inch cuts and add to a large pot with the garlic, onions, bay leaves and thyme.

2. Fill to about an inch and a half with water then add salt and black pepper to season well.
3. Allow to boil then reduce to a simmer, skimming the top of scum. Simmer for an hour so that meats become tender.
4. Take out bay leaves and the thyme then strain off broth to keep.
5. Grind the pork and liver with the cooked garlic and onion or finely chop by hand.

To prepare the rice

1. Bring three cups of the broth to a boil in a pot, and the rice and more salt and pepper as needed.
2. Turn down low heat, cover and cook for another 20 minutes to complete the rice.
3. Add the cooked rice to the ground meat along with the parsley and green onions. Mix well.
4. Season salt, black and cayenne peppers.
5. Form into flattened patties or rounded balls and fry.

Pairs well with – bread, pickled okra, potatoes

84. Chatrou

The most common way to prepare this small octopus is to do a fricassee. The tentacles are cut into pieces and prepared with lime or lemon juice then stewed down with tomatoes and seasonings. This soft meaty stew is served well with rice and beans.

Serves 4

Ingredients

2 lb Chatrou tentacles
1 onion
2 garlic cloves
4 stalks green onions
4 sprigs parsley
1 vegetarian chilli pepper
2 whole cloves
2 tomatoes
1 sprig thyme
2 limes
2 cups sunflower oil

Preparation
1. Clean and rinse the octopus with water then rub with one lime.
2. Cut up the tentacles into little pieces.
3. Put some water in a sauce pan to boil, add the octopus and boil for five minutes.
4. Drain and retain the water from boiling.
5. Chop the onions, garlic, green onions, parsley and tomatoes.

6. Heat some of the oil in a pan and add the chopped seasonings, as well as the cloves for 2 minutes.
7. Add some of the broth to the pan and also the chilli pepper.
8. Add the contents of that pan to a pressure cooker along with the octopus, cover and cook for forty minutes on a low flame.
9. Take lid off and cook uncovered for 10 minutes to allow sauce to thicken.
10. Add some lime juice when cooking is complete.

Pairs well with – rice and kidney beans

85. Colombo

Colombo is actually a combination of spices out of East and West India and France. The spice contains turmeric, coriander, brown mustard seeds, bay leaves, hot pepper, thyme and pepper corns. It can be purchased pre-made at local stores. This recipe uses the Colombo powder to prepare chicken but it can also be used on other meats and also vegetables.

Serves 6

Ingredients

2 tbsp sunflower oil
1 tbsp butter
1 cut up chicken
4 tbsp Colombo powder
16 oz chicken broth
2 cup chopped onions
14 oz coconut milk
1 crushed clove garlic
2 tbsp lime juice, fresh
2 tbsp fresh thyme leaves
2 tbsp chopped green onions
3 tbsp parsley, chopped
1 tsp chopped scotch bonnet
1 tbsp salt
1 tbsp pepper
1/2 cup pistachios (shelled, optional)

Preparation

1. Heat the oil and the butter in a large pot and add in the chicken and Colombo seasoning. Cook on a medium flame for fifteen minutes until browned.
2. Add half the coconut milk and other ingredients leaving the pistachios out and simmer for three quarters of an hour on a medium flame.
3. Turn off, then add the rest of the coconut milk and the pistachios. Stir them in and serve.

Pairs well with - Creole rice

86. Lambis

The sea snail, lambis or conch is another popular food in Martinique. This recipe presents as a stew but can also be grilled or fried, made into a casserole, or even a pancake.

Serves 4

Ingredients

2 lb lambis
1 lime
1 lemon
3 tbsp olive oil
2 tsps vinegar
2 large diced tomatoes
1 shallot
2 minced cloves garlic
1 diced medium onion
2 tsps margarine
4 cup water
olive oil
hot pepper
salt and black pepper
1 tbsp tomato paste

Preparation

1. Clean the conch with the juice from the lime and the lemon and rinse with boiling water.
2. Retain the pink portions and cut up the very thick pieces.

3. Boil them in 32 ounces of water for no less than 2 hours, skimming scum at intervals. Retain the broth.
4. Remove the conch and brown the pieces in a pan with butter and oil as well as a couple drops of the lime juice.
5. Add the remaining ingredients then add 16 ounces of the retained broth. Simmer for a short while then add more salt and pepper as desired.

Pairs well with - rice with red beans

87. Le Matautou de Crabe

It is common for Martinicans to have this dish during the Lenten season using mangrove or land crabs. It is not uncommon for locals to obtain the crabs weeks in advance of the season and feed them with a specific diet of vegetables and different spices in preparation.

Serves 2

Ingredients

8 oz crabmeat
1 tbsp lemon or lime juice
3 scallions
½ tbsp finely chopped chives
2 medium sized shallots (sliced)
1 tbsp chopped parsley
2 thyme sprigs
1 tbsp salt
Black pepper
2 minced garlic cloves
2 or 3 large tomatoes (deseeded and cut in four)
2 ½ tbsp olive oil
3 cloves
2 bay leaves
¼ tsp hot pepper (if desired)
2 cup cooked rice

Preparation

1. Add lemon juice to the crab and put aside.
2. Sauté all the seasonings in oil for two minutes then add the crab and cook for another five to seven minutes.
3. Add the rice, simmer for four minutes and serve hot.

Pairs well with – spicy sauce

88. Le Feroce d'Avocat

This recipe literally means fierce avocado, which refers to the pepper content of this dish. In the days of slavery, it served as a breakfast meal for sugar plantation workers. Today, it widely includes salt fish but may also come in variations which use lobster or crab. This is a truly spicy guacamole with a difference.

Serves 6

Ingredients

½ lb desalted cod fish
1 large ripened avocado or 2 medium sized avocados
½ lb cassava flour
3 scallions
2 habañero peppers
3 crushed garlic cloves
½ bunch parsley
3 tbsp sunflower oil
1 squeezed lime
Pepper
Salt

Preparation

1. To desalt the cod fish, boil some water in a pot with the fish in it, drain, flake then set aside.
2. Slice the avocado in two and cut the flesh into chunks.

3. Sprinkle some lime juice over the chunks to prevent oxidation.
4. Finely chop the parsley then add the avocado, fish, garlic, scallions and a small piece of the pepper.
5. Mix well, adding the cassava flour and oil during mixing.
6. Add some salt and pepper to taste and refrigerate for at least an hour prior to serving.

Pairs well with – fried green plantains

Montserrat

89. Goat Water

Far from being watery, goat water is a rich well flavored stew. The traditional method of preparation is over an outdoor wood fire which adds a smoky dimension to the flavor. Interestingly, some people add a small amount of scotch or rum to their preparation to aid the flavor.

Serves 12

Ingredients

2 goat quarters
4 cut up onions
Escallions and thyme
2 tbsp ketchup
1 whole green hot pepper
salt and pepper
4 minced cloves garlic
1 tbsp crushed cloves
1 tbsp grated nutmeg or mace
6 oz cooking oil
3 oz marjoram
2 cup flour
Gravy browning
Scotch or rum (if desired)

Preparation
1. Cube the goat meat into 2 inch pieces with the bones intact then wash with salted water.
2. Put the meat in a large stewing pot and cover the pieces with water and boil.
3. Simmer with the lid on for five minutes, skimming the foam.
4. Add all the ingredients up to the marjoram and add more hot water if needed.
5. After about two hours, make a white wash with the flour and add it for thickness, stirring while adding.
6. Add browning at this point to enhance the color.
7. Place the lid halfway over the mouth of the pot and simmer until completely cooked. Add a little rum or scotch if desired.

Pairs well with - bread

Netherlands

90. Pannenkoeken

This simple recipe makes very tasty traditional Dutch pancakes. They are much larger than regular pancakes and much flatter. They can be compared to crepes but are slightly thicker. Although widely known as a breakfast food, Dutch natives tend to have these at lunch or dinner time. Fillings can be incorporated during cooking.

Serves 6 to 8

Ingredients

2 cups self-raising flour
1 teaspoon salt
1 egg
2 cups milk
Margarine or butter

Preparation

1. Mix the flour with the salt and make a well in the centre.
2. Add the egg along with half the milk and mix into a batter.
3. Gradually stir and add the rest of the milk. Rest the batter for 30 minutes.
4. Heat a little butter in a skillet then pour just enough batter to make a thin layer in the pan.

5. Cook on medium heat until the top dries out then flip and cook the next side. It is ready when it turns golden brown. Serve warm.

Pairs well with – Stroop or brown sugar

91. Erwtensoep

Erwtensoep is a traditional Dutch pea soup which is also very popular in the winter. This hearty soup can be varied as desired as long as at least 500 grams of split peas are included for each litre of water used. Some prefer it extremely thick while other Dutch natives will go for a less thick consistency.

Serves 4 to 6

Ingredients

10 ½ oz dried green split peas
3 ½ oz thick sliced bacon
1 pork chop (5 or 6 oz)
1 stock cube
2 sticks celery
3 ½ oz sliced carrots
1 large potato (cubed and peeled)
1 small chopped onion
1 small sliced leek
3 ½ oz cubed celeriac
Salt and pepper
Handful of celery leaves (chopped)
Handful smoked sausage (sliced)

Preparation

1. Boil 1 ¾ litres of water in a large pot and add the bacon, split peas and pork. Skim away any froth during boiling then place lid on top. Boil gently for ¾ hour stirring intermittently.

2. Remove the pork chop, debone, slice thinly then set aside for later addition.
3. Add all of the vegetables and cook for a further half an hour. Add some water every now and again to prevent the soup from catching.
4. Add the sausage, 15 minutes into the half hour.
5. Remove both the bacon and smoked sausage once the vegetables are cooked. Slice them thinly and reserve.
6. You may puree the soup or have it as is, adding salt and pepper then the meats. Reserve some of the sausage.
7. Use the celery leaves and sausage slices to garnish.

Pairs well with – bread, bread and butter or cream cheese and chive brood

Puerto Rico

92. Mofongo

This Puerto Rican staple is an interesting fried mashed plantain which serves as a side dish for many entrees.

Serves 4

Ingredients

4 green plantains
2 cup olive oil (canola oil)
Salt to taste
6 cloves garlic
2 tbsp extra virgin olive oil
1 lb crispy fried pork rinds
1 slice cooked bacon
8 oz chicken stock (low sodium)

Preparation

1. Peel then slice the plantains into 1" rounds.
2. Fry the plantains in very hot oil for a total of seven minutes, both sides. Drain excess oil using paper towels.
3. Using a large pestle and mortar, crush the garlic with salt then add olive oil pounding well. Place in a small dish.

4. Crush half the plantains in the mortar along with half the pork rinds, half the bacon and half of the previously crushed garlic.
5. Add half of the chicken stock if necessary to moisten.
6. Make 2" balls from the mash and keep warm until serving time.
7. Remember to mash the remaining half of the fried plantains in a similar manner.

Pairs well with – salad or rice and beans

93. Chicken Asopao

This hearty one dish meal is a traditional Puerto Rican fixing. It is chock full of flavor with chicken, olives, garlic, onions, rice and pepper flakes. It is a very thick stew and goes wonderfully with avocado slices.

Serves 6

Ingredients

2 lb chicken thighs (bones and skins removed)
½ tsp black pepper
1 adobo seasoning sachet
3 tbsp olive oil
1 diced green bell pepper
1 diced medium onion
4 minced garlic gloves
2 tbsp tomato paste
1 ½ cup rice
14 ½ oz diced canned tomatoes
6 cup chicken broth (low sodium)
1 bay leaf
¼ tsp red pepper flakes
1 cup petite peas (frozen kind but thawed)
1 cup sliced green olives (with pimentos)
¼ cup fresh cilantro (chopped)

Preparation

1. Use the adobo seasoning and black pepper to rub the chicken well.

2. Cook the peppers, onions, garlic and tomato paste in hot oil then put aside.
3. Brown the thighs on either side by frying then add the cooked vegetables, rice, tomatoes, broth, bay leaf, and pepper flakes.
4. Allow to boil then lower flame to allow contents to simmer for twenty minutes.
5. Add the peas and sliced olives then continue cooking for five more minutes. Turn flame off and remove bay leaf.
6. Add in the cilantro then serve.

Pairs well with – sliced avocado, cilantro

94. Puerto Rican Roasted Pork

This well-flavored pork shoulder is also called Pernil. In other parts of the region it is served as a special occasion meal typically at Christmas and New Year. The leftovers are used to make sandwiches.

Serves 8

Ingredients

2 oz olive oil
3 tbsp vinegar
10 garlic cloves (or more)
2 tbsp oregano flakes
1 tbsp salt
1 ½ tsps black pepper
5 lb pork shoulder (extra fat removed)

Preparation

1. Meld all the ingredients except the pork together in a mortar and pestle.
2. Making slits into the pork using a knife, push the paste down into the holes then rub the remainder all over the meat.
3. Put the pork inside a plastic roasting bag, rest in roasting pan with rack and marinate in fridge for between 8 hours and 2 days.

4. Bring the pork to room temperature before serving. Perhaps for an hour or two.
5. Set the oven to 300 °F or 150 °C.
6. Rest the pork on the side with the skin on the rack in the roasting pan for two hours. It will become golden brown.
7. Turn on the other side and roast until the juices run clear, in about two to four hours. An internal thermometer should read about 145 °F or 63 C when it is ready.

Pairs well with – salad, rice and beans, sweet plantains

95. Arroz con Pollo

This highly aromatic rice and chicken meal is quite simple to prepare and is quite flavorful. It is much more than a simple rice with chicken dish. It is a beautiful saffron color which makes it even more appealing to the senses and pleasing to the eyes.

Serves 4

Ingredients

3 cup rinsed rice
2 lb chicken parts (skin removed)
4 ½ oz tomato sauce
2 tbsp alcaparrado
Salt
½ tsp black pepper
2 tbsp Sofrito
2 tbsp vegetable oil
4 cup of boiling water
1 sazon with saffron sachet

Preparation

1. In a very big dutch oven, brown the pieces of chicken for five minutes on either side, using the oil.
2. Set the chicken aside once finished and add the other ingredients but not the rice and water to the drippings.

3. Mix them well cooking the sofrito for at least five minutes. Taste for salt.
4. Now add the browned chicken as well as the rice and mix.
5. Add the hot water to an inch above the level of the rice and mix.
6. Cook with the pot open and all the water dries off.
7. Use a wooden spoon to stir the contents from bottom to top then put lid on and cook on a low flame for about 20 or 25 minutes for the rice to become tender.

Pairs well with – green beans, steamed vegetables

Saint Barthelemy (St. Barths)

96. Feroce D'Avocat

This spicy avocado dip is a French recipe with a Caribbean twist owing to the addition of cod fish. The use of an entire hot pepper gives you an idea of the level of zing you can expect to encounter. Some people choose to balance that with a little sugar.

Serves 2

Ingredients

1 ripened avocado
5 oz codfish, soaked for two days to remove salt
1 herbal bouquet
Juice of a lemon
1 thinly sliced hot pepper
Salt and pepper

Preparation

1. Cook the fish for fifteen minutes with the herbal bouquet then cool and flake.
2. Remove the avocado peel and mash the flesh with a fork.

3. Add the fish, lemon juice, salt and pepper and pepper slices to the mashed avocado.
4. Garnish with fresh parsley and serve.

Pairs well with – fried green plantains, tomato slices

97. Mahi Mahi

The mahi mahi is a very fleshy fish and absorbs the seasonings and spices used on it exceptionally well. This mahi mahi has braised garlic, chives, herbs and roucou oil extracted from the annatto plant.

Serves 4

Ingredients

5 mahi-mahi steaks
1/3 parsley bouquet
1 onion
4 garlic cloves
3 chives
5 bouquets of herbs
3 well ripe tomatoes
1 tbsp roucou oil
Juice from a lemon
Salt

Preparation

1. Brown sliced herbs and the tomatoes in the oil in a large pot with the lid on.
2. Once the tomatoes and herbs become soft, add in the fish along with salt.

3. Cover the fish with hot water, place the lid on and cook on low for twenty minutes.
4. Add lemon juice to serve.

Pairs well with - white rice, polenta, hot chilli pepper

St. Kitts and Nevis

98. Coconut Dumplings

These coconut dumplings comprise part of the national dish of St. Kitts and Nevis which also includes stewed salt fish, seasoned breadfruit and spicy plantains. They are very simple to make and are boiled and not fried.

Serves 4

Ingredients

½ cup grated coconut
1 ½ cup flour
¼ teaspoon salt
3 tsps oil
1 tablespoon margarine
4 oz water

Preparation

1. Put the coconut, salt, oil, flour and margarine into a dish.
2. Add the water little by little to form a firm dough.
3. Knead on a lightly floured surface for only 2 minutes then shape the dumplings.

4. Place them into salted boiling water and cook for about 15 minutes.

Pairs well with – stewed salt fish, seasoned breadfruit, spicy plantains

99. Seasoned Breadfruit

This breadfruit dish represents a quarter of the national dish of St. Kitts and Nevis. It is nicely seasoned with chicken broth, thyme, garlic and onions and is so well flavored that it can be had on its own. It is however made much better with the national accompaniments.

Serves 4

Ingredients

3 cup full breadfruit (cut into 1" cubes)
2 tbsp oil
1 tablespoon unsalted butter
½ cup diced red pepper
1 medium chopped onion
4 crushed garlic cloves
2 tbsp chopped fresh parsley
1 tablespoon thyme leaves
4 oz chicken broth
¼ tablespoon salt
¼ teaspoon ground pepper

Preparation

1. Melt the butter in a thick bottomed saucepan then add the oil.
2. Sauté the onions for between five and eight minutes, while stirring.
3. Add the garlic, pepper, thyme and parsley, cooking for only half a minute.

4. Remove from the flame and add the breadfruit and broth, gently tossing to blend well.
5. Season with the salt and pepper then serve.

Pairs well with – dumplings, salt fish, spicy plantain

100. Conch Salad

The strong citrus flavor from the lime or lemon juice coupled with the spicy heat from the red peppers makes this salad burst with flavor in your mouth. The greens reds and whites provided by the various vegetables as well as the conch makes for a very attractive presentation.

Serves 8 to 10

Ingredients

2 finely chopped celery stalks
1 finely chopped medium onion
2 finely chopped green peppers
2 ripe firm tomatoes, diced
2 finely chopped hot red peppers
4 oz lime or lemon juice
1 peeled and diced small cucumber
3 lb finely diced conch
Salt

Preparation

1. Thoroughly wash the conch in two big bowls of salted water. Soak for a half an hour in the second bowl.
2. Drain away any excess salt water and mix all the ingredients together in a good-sized bowl.
3. Place in the fridge for an hour or so and serve chilled.

Pairs well with – lettuce, beer, sky juice

St. Lucia

101. Breadfruit Pie

Breadfruit pie is a lovely savoury dish with layers of onions and breadfruit baked together with a creamy cheese sauce. It is a delectable side and fills a similar slot as macaroni pie would.

Serves 6

Ingredients

1 full breadfruit
10 oz cheddar cheese soup
8 oz milk
1 onion
Salt and pepper
½ cup fine breadcrumbs
½ cup grated cheese
¼ cup butter

Preparation

1. Cut the breadfruit into eight sections and boil in water to which salt was added, until just tender.
2. Heat the oven beforehand to 350 °F.
3. Mix the cheese soup and milk together.

4. Thinly slice the breadfruit and onion.
5. Layer the breadfruit and onion, one after the other in a greased pyrex dish.
6. Pour the cheese sauce over the breadfruit and onion layers.
7. Place dots of butter on top.
8. Mix the breadcrumbs and cheese together and sprinkle on top of the pie. Bake for about three quarters of an hour. Serve while still hot.

Pairs well with – baked chicken, stewed fish

102. Greenfig Salad

This salad easily takes the place of a potato salad with its creamy texture and colorful hues. Most versions have codfish flakes added although this one does not. You may add it if you so desire. Other versions can also include chicken or turkey breast.

Serves 4

Ingredients

1 lime
1 tbsp oil
2 diced sweet peppers (red and green)
1 diced onion
6 green bananas
1 boiled egg, diced
Mayonnaise
Salt and pepper

Preparation:

1. Score the green bananas then boil them in water to which the oil and lime juice has been added.
2. Peel and dice the bananas when cool and place in a dish with the other ingredients.
3. Toss together and serve.

Pairs well with – escoveitched fish and tossed salad

St. Martin & St. Maarten

103. Rum Barbecue Sauce

This origin of this recipe is Southern in nature. A traditional recipe would have bourbon instead of rum and Worcestershire sauce instead of Pickapeppa sauce. This Caribbean spin on a southern oldie does reveal that substitution can be just as spectacular as the original.

Makes 10 oz

Ingredients

6 oz tomato paste
1/3 cap full dark rum
2 oz white vinegar
2 oz molasses
2 crushed garlic cloves
3 tsps Pickapeppa Sauce
13 tsps soy sauce (low sodium)
¼ tsp hot sauce

Preparation

1. Blend all the ingredients in a food processor for about two minutes.

2. Pour into a small saucepan and boil quickly to prevent caramelization.
3. Cool and store in a tightly covered jar and keep in the fridge.

Pairs well with – baked chicken, roasted meats

104. Jerked King Fish

The signature of anything jerked is the smoked flavor. These king fish steaks are jerked over coals which imparts the smoky character, which marries perfectly with the jerk marinade.

Serves 6

Ingredients

6 8oz, kingfish steaks
4 oz lime juice
3 oz jerk marinade

Preparation

1. Wash the fish steaks with the lime juice, rinse and dry.
2. In a shallow container pour the jerk marinade over them and turn to coat both sides.
3. Take fish out of marinade and save marinade for later.
4. Cook the fish over heated coals on a grill for about five minutes on either side, basting with the marinade in between. Serve when finished.

Pairs well with – Hard dough bread and beer

St. Vincent & The Grenadines

105. Stuffed Sweet Potatoes

Without any additional ingredients, these stuffed sweet potatoes have the right goodness for them to be considered a balanced meal. The sweetness of the potatoes and corn with the saltiness of the bacon makes for a delicious and filling dish.

Serves 2 to 4

Ingredients

2 lb sweet potatoes
Vegetable oil
4 slices bacon
½ cup cooked meat, diced
½ cup sweet corn
1 medium onion, diced
1 tbsp margarine
Salt and pepper

Preparation

1. Thoroughly scrub the potatoes then dry them and brush them with oil.
2. Put them on a baking tray and bake at 400 ºF for an hour and a half.

3. Fry the bacon and onions until the bacon is crispy and the onions are translucent.
4. Halve the baked potatoes, scoop the middles out and roughly chop the flesh.
5. Mix in the butter, bacon and onions, corn and salt and pepper and mix well.
6. Spoon the mixture into the potato skins and heat again in the oven for 15 minutes.

Pairs well with – chilli, garlic butter

106. Green Pigeon Peas Soup

This soup has many different versions across the Caribbean. In Jamaica it is called gungo peas soup and pigeon peas soup everywhere else. Regardless of the variation, the deliciousness of the Caribbean flavors is sure to emerge.

Serves 6

Ingredients

2 cup green pigeon peas
1 oz margarine
½ lb soup meat
1 large onion
6 cup water
2 sprigs of celery
Salt and pepper
6 oz pumpkin
1 lb tannias
1 green plantain
Dumplings (flour water and salt to form a stiff dough)
3 tbsp oil
1 large sliced carrot

Preparation

1. Chop the celery, onions and pumpkin and cut up the meat into small cubes.

2. Heat the oil in a sauce pan and sauté the seasonings and pumpkin.
3. Add the meat and fry until brown.
4. Add the peas and some water and cook until the peas are splitting and soft. Add hot water as needed to make up the volume of soup.
5. Peel the carrots, plantain and tannias and cut them all into small pieces.
6. Add them to the soup along with salt and pepper to balance the taste.
7. Make the dumplings and form them into flattened balls or logs and add to the soup when almost cooked.
8. Add butter along with the dumplings and check the taste adjusting if necessary.

Pairs well with - bread or rolls

Trinidad & Tobago

107. Cow Heel Soup

Cow heel or cow foot soup is a hearty soup which is made right across the Caribbean. It contains vegetables, pepper and dumplings and of course the cow heels which get gelatinous upon cooking.

Serves 8

Ingredients

2 lb cow heel cut into small pieces
1 tsp salt
1 whole scotch bonnet pepper
2 cut up carrots
3 potatoes
1 cup yellow split peas
4 thyme sprig
2 stalks scallion
1 tbsp vegetable oil
8 to 10 Okras
½ tsp black pepper
4 dried pimento berries
1 large diced onion
2 garlic cloves
12 to16 cup water
1 cup diced pumpkin

For Dumplings
1 C flour
pinch salt
water

Preparation

1. Using a deep sauce pan heat the oil and add the diced onion, diced garlic, pimento, thyme sprigs and black pepper for about five minutes.
2. Add the cow heel and stir then add the split peas, carrots and salt and add water to cover the ingredients.
3. Turn the heat up to boil then turn down and simmer. Allow to cook for 2 to 2½ hours or pressure for half an hour.
4. Add the whole pepper when the soup starts to simmer. Skim any scum off the top off the soup.
5. When the cow heels are cooked add the okras, potatoes, scallions and pumpkin. Cook for another half an hour.
6. Make the dumplings by adding a pinch of salt to the flour and a little water to make a firm dough. Rest them for fifteen minutes and add to the soup in the final ten cooking minutes.
7. Roll them into little cigar shapes or spinners and add to the soup.
8. Taste and add salt as needed.

Pairs well with – white rice

108. Curry Mango

This recipe makes use of green mangoes which makes a delicious dish for vegetarians or serves as an accompaniment to meat dishes. This combination gives you sweet, tang, spice and saltiness all at the same time.

Serves 6

Ingredients

4 or 5 green mangoes
2 tbsp Trinidadian curry powder
8 oz water
1 tbsp vegetable oil
2 cloves shredded garlic
1 tsp salt
2 tbsp sugar
West Indian hot pepper sauce
2 tsps Anchar massala (or garram massala)

Preparation

1. Wash, peel and cut the mangoes into lengthwise pieces yielding 6 or 8 pieces each and set aside.
2. Make a paste with the curry powder in half cup water.
3. Use a heavy pot to heat the oil and cook the curry paste with constant stirring on a low flame for one minute.

4. Add the peeled mangoes and stir then add the rest of the water, salt, garlic, sugar and pepper.
5. Turn the flame down and put the lid on the pot, cooking the mangoes until they become tender and the liquid has dried down.
6. If too sour add more sugar and sprinkle on some anchar massala and stir thoroughly.
7. Turn off the heat and add salt and pepper as needed.

Pairs well with – white rice

109. Baighan Chokha

This roasted eggplant dish has East Indian roots and is a savoury side dish which pairs well with many entrees. In the middle east it is known as baba ganush but has the same garlicy flavor.

Serves 4

Ingredients

2 medium sized baigan (eggplant)
2 garlic cloves
½ finely chopped onion
3 tbsp oil
Salt

Preparation

1. Slightly oil the outside of the eggplant and slowly roast it by hand over a stove, slowly rotating it until the skin starts to thin.
2. Remove from stove and rest on a paper towel.
3. Cut lengthwise and remove the flesh with a spoon and keep it in a dish. Discard the skin.
4. Crush the flesh until smooth and add a finely chopped garlic clove and the onions.

5. Fry the remaining garlic clove until golden and add it with the oil into the mashed baigan.
6. Add some salt and also pepper if you so desire and mix well.

Pairs well with – sada roti

110. Pholourie

This fried snack is an excellent addition to any meal either as an appetizer or as a snack option. It pairs well with tangy tamarind sauce however the oil content can be a little high, so you can try placing them in the oven to reduce the amount of oil. When cooked, Pholourie are soft and fluffy on the inside but slightly crispy on the outside.

Serves 8 to 10

Ingredients

4 cups flour
10 chadon beni leaves, minced
5 small garlic cloves, minced
1 small hot pepper, minced
½ teaspoon saffron powder
1 teaspoon yeast
1 teaspoon salt
8 oz water
½ teaspoon baking powder
Oil to fry

Preparation

1. Mix the flour with the yeast and baking powder then add the saffron and salt and combine well.
2. Combine the chadon beni, pepper, minced garlic and water in another container.

3. Add 3 tablespoons of the latter mixture to the flour a small portion at a time, stirring with each addition and until completed. Leave to rise for one hour.
4. Drop the batter into hot oil to fry using a tablespoon for each one. Always dip the spoon in water before dipping into the batter.
5. Remove when a slight brown color appears and drain oil on absorbent paper towel.

Pairs well with – tamarind sauce, chadon beni chutney, mango chutney

111. Macaroni Pie

This dish is well known across the world but every nation has its own particular method of preparing it. Some people add meat based fillings, some add vegetables, while others maintain it pure and unadulterated. A major advantage is that it is easy to prepare.

Serves 8

Ingredients

20 oz macaroni
1 egg
2 to 3 tsps tomato paste
2 tbsp butter
6 oz evaporated milk
1 lb grated cheese
1 small finely grated onion
1 dried pimento berry
1 teaspoon parsley flakes
1 chopped sprig chive
½ teaspoon paprika
1 teaspoon bitters
favorite powdered seasonings
Salt and pepper sauce

Preparation

1. Boil the macaroni for only ten minutes then drain and add butter.

2. Add the milk, egg, cheese and tomato paste and mix everything well.
3. Add the herbs, bitters, seasonings and pepper sauce and mix once again.
4. Pour the mixture into a greased pyrex dish and spread some cheese on top.
5. Bake at 350 °F for half an hour. The top will become golden brown.

Pairs well with – fried fish, baked chicken

Turks & Caicos Islands

112. Ginger Mango Chicken

This creamy chicken creation has an amazing flavor when coupled with the ginger and garlic, in addition to the sweetness contributed by the mango chutney. It also has a beautiful golden color from the coating and a slightly crispy outside.

Servings: 6

Ingredients

6 8 oz chicken breasts, bones removed
Garlic powder
Salt and black pepper
8 oz evaporated milk
1 egg
1 cup flour
2 cup breadcrumbs
mango chutney

Preparation

1. Heat the oven to 350 °F.
2. lb the chicken breasts with a mallet then season with salt, pepper and garlic powder.

3. Add some chutney to one half of the flattened chicken breast then fold.
4. Dip in flour, milk, beaten egg then bread crumbs
5. Brown chicken in a frying pan with hot oil then flip and repeat for the other side.
6. Drain the extra oil on a paper towel then bake in the oven for twenty-five minutes.

Pairs well with – rice and beans, steamed vegetables, green salad

113. Fish Batter

Fish batter is a delicious and crispy lunch item which can also be had for a light dinner. It is popular in restaurants in the Turks and Caicos Islands and is served most often with fries. The thick batter helps the fish retain its moist juiciness on the inside.

Serves 4 to 6

Ingredients

3 cup Soybean oil
2 lbs cod fillets
1 cup self-raising flour
1/3 cup dry mustard
8 oz water
1 Egg
2 tsps granulated sugar
2 tsps salt

Preparation

1. Slice the fish into long wedges.
2. Sift the dry mustard and flour together then blend them with water, sugar, the egg and salt.
3. Heat the oil to 400 °F in a deep frying pan.
4. Coat each fillet generously with the batter and fry until dark brown. Drain on paper towels.

Pairs well with – green beans, lemon wedges, fries, tartar sauce

US Virgin Islands

114. Crab & Rice

Crab and rice is the perfect dish for crab lovers because it offers a way to eat the entire crab along with rice. Not just the meat but also the crab shell pieces with the meat inside are included. This is a 'put your fork down and eat with your hands' type of dish which will have you licking your fingers.

Serves 4

Ingredients

6 to 8 crabs
1 large onion
1 small sweet pepper
1 cup boiled pigeon peas
2 cup rice
3 to 4 tbsp tomato paste
Salt and pepper
Paprika
Thyme to taste

Preparation

1. Wash the crabs, remove the claws and set them aside.
2. Remove the bodies from the backs and scoop the fat out into a bowl.

3. Crack the bodies into different sections, beat them as well as the claws and put aside.
4. Chop the onion and sweet pepper and sauté until soft.
5. Add in tomato paste, seasonings and crab fat and simmer for 5 minutes.
6. Add 24 ounces of water and boil then add the peas and crab pieces and allow to boil again.
7. After five minutes add the rice, bring to boil again and then turn down to simmer until the rice cooks.

Pairs well with – sliced cucumbers, lemon wedges

115. Stuffed Eggplant

This hollowed out eggplant recipe contains a complete meal with the eggplant flesh, rice and cooked meat. The oregano and thyme leaves along with the parmesan cheese give it an Italian essence.

Serves 1

Ingredients

1 Eggplant
½ cup cooked rice
¾ cup cooked meat (or fish, vegetables or tofu)
2 tbsp butter
1 tomato, chopped
½ onion, chopped
½ bell pepper, chopped
1 tsp thyme leaves
1 tsp oregano flakes
2 tbsp water
Salt and pepper
3/4 cup bread crumbs
1/4 cup Parmesan cheese

Preparation

1. Cut the eggplant along its length and slice the top off.
2. Scoop the pulp out, dice it and put in a dish.
3. Melt the butter in a skillet and sauté the eggplant flesh with the tomatoes, onions and bell peppers until soft.

4. Add some water, the meat, cooked rice, thyme leaves and oregano flakes to continue sautéing for a few minutes more.
5. Add salt and pepper.
6. Put the hollowed-out shells into the oven set at 350 °F for 10 minutes.
7. Spoon the rice mixture into the shells and sprinkle with a mixture of breadcrumbs and Parmesan.
8. Bake at 400 °F for about 20 minutes.

Pairs well with – asparagus and herbed tomatoes

Caribbean Tools & Utensils

Whilst preparing and cooking your Caribbean meals, you may want the assistance of the correct utensils. The table below lists the utensils that will greatly help achieve the Caribbean dishes that you desire.

Utensil	Description	Use
Dutch Pot / Oven	A strong cast iron cooking pot with thick walls	Used for cooking meats, stews, soups and rice
Mortar and Pestle	Small ceramic or stainless steel bowl with blunt crushing instrument	For grinding and crushing herbs and spices into paste
Calabash Bowl	Large bowl made of hardwood	Used for serving
Wooden Spoon	Large bamboo spoon	Used for serving
Knife Set	A professional knife set with various sizes	Needed for slicing of meat and vegetables
Caribbean Cookware Set	A complete set of dutch pot, skillet and sauce pan	For all food cooking

Conclusion

I hope you have enjoyed this culinary adventure through the 26 beautiful and idyllic Caribbean islands. You now have experience of the fusion of cultures from all over the world and within the region that contributes to the diversity of flavors in Caribbean cuisine. Truly a melting pot of global cuisines, the Caribbean has so much to offer. Even though we have covered 115 recipes, we have still only just scratched the surface.

Please share these recipes with your family and friends and excite them with the Caribbean vibe!

If you have a craving for more Caribbean recipes then be sure to check out my other books and gain further skills to add to your repertoire:

Just a reminder…don't forget to visit **www.ffdrecipes.com** for your FREE bonus cookbooks and to get exclusive access to our World Recipes Club, which provides FREE book offers, discounts and recipe ideas!

Thank you.

Cooking Measurements & Conversions

Oven Temperature Conversions

Use the below table as a guide to establishing the correct temperatures when cooking, however please be aware that oven types and models and location of your kitchen can have an influence on temperature also.

°F	°C	Gas Mark	Explanation
275°F	140°C	1	cool
300°F	150°C	2	
325°F	170°C	3	very moderate
350°F	180°C	4	moderate
375°F	190°C	5	
400°F	200°C	6	moderately hot
425°F	220°C	7	hot
450°F	230°C	8	
475°F	240°C	9	very hot

US to Metric Corresponding Measures

Metric	Imperial
3 teaspoons	1 tablespoon
1 tablespoon	1/16 cup
2 tablespoons	1/8 cup
2 tablespoons + 2 teaspoons	1/6 cup
4 tablespoons	1/4 cup
5 tablespoons + 1 teaspoon	1/3 cup
6 tablespoons	3/8 cup
8 tablespoons	1/2 cup
10 tablespoons + 2 teaspoons	2/3 cup
12 tablespoons	3/4 cup
16 tablespoons	1 cup
48 teaspoons	1 cup

8 fluid ounces (fl oz)	1 cup
1 pint	2 cups
1 quart	2 pints
1 quart	4 cups
1 gallon (gal)	4 quarts
1 cubic centimeter (cc)	1 milliliter (ml)
2.54 centimeters (cm)	1 inch (in)
1 pound (lb)	16 ounces (oz)

Liquid to Volume

Metric	Imperial
15ml	1 tbsp
55 ml	2 fl oz
75 ml	3 fl oz
150 ml	5 fl oz (¼ pint)
275 ml	10 fl oz (½ pint)
570 ml	1 pint
725 ml	1 ¼ pints
1 litre	1 ¾ pints
1.2 litres	2 pints
1.5 litres	2½ pints
2.25 litres	4 pints

Weight Conversion

Metric	Imperial
10 g	½ oz
20 g	¾ oz
25 g	1 oz
40 g	1½ oz
50 g	2 oz
60 g	2½ oz
75 g	3 oz
110 g	4 oz
125 g	4½ oz
150 g	5 oz
175 g	6 oz
200 g	7 oz
225 g	8 oz
250 g	9 oz
275 g	10 oz

350 g	12 oz
450 g	1 lb
700 g	1 lb 8 oz
900 g	2 lb
1.35 kg	3 lb

Cooking Abbreviations

Abbreviation	Description
tsp	teaspoon
Tbsp	tablespoon
c	cup
pt	pint
qt	quart
gal	gallon
wt	weight
oz	ounce
lb	pound
g	gram
kg	kilogram
vol	volume
ml	milliliter
fl oz	fluid ounce

Special Request...

As you can tell, I'm passionate about Caribbean food and eager to share this wonderful cuisine with as many people as I can. If you don't mind, I'd like to ask you for your help to enable more people to discover the food we love.

I'm seeking feedback from readers and I would greatly appreciate it if you would leave a review. I really value your opinion!

To leave a review, simply visit the link below:

http://hyperurl.co/115CaribbeanReview

Again, I really appreciate you taking the time to read the book and provide feedback!

Thank you very much.

Made in United States
North Haven, CT
26 September 2022